Jim shares witty wisdom based on God's timeless principles as revealed in the Bible. We who are "over the hill" are headed for the mountaintop, and that's something to celebrate! A must-read for anyone who suspects they might be aging.

RACHAEL PHILIPPS, award-winning humor columnist

A humorous guide to staying young while growing old. Brilliant!

DAVID L. WINTERS, author of *Exercising Your Faith*

The book's encouraging Scriptures, helpful quotations, godly wisdom, and laugh-out-loud hilarity helped me believe that I could remain a fun person as I aged—even if I buy Tums by the bucket.

JEANETTE LEVELLIE, *Guideposts* writer and author of *The Heart of Humor*

If You're Not Dead, You're Not Done

LIVE WITH PURPOSE AT ANY AGE

JAMES N. WATKINS

Tyndale House Publishers
Carol Stream, Illinois

LIVING
EXPRESSIONS
® COLLECTION

Living Expressions invites you to explore
God's Word in a way that is refreshing to
your spirit and restorative to your soul.

Visit Tyndale online at tyndale.com.

TYNDALE, Tyndale's quill logo, *Living Expressions*, and the Living Expressions logo are registered trademarks of Tyndale House Ministries.

If You're Not Dead, You're Not Done: Live with Purpose at Any Age

Designed by Libby Dykstra

Edited by Bonne Steffen

Quotations from Thomas à Kempis are taken from *The Imitation of Christ: Classic Devotions in Today's Language*, compiled and edited by James N. Watkins (Nashville: Hachette Book Group, 2015).

Chapters 1 and 11 adapted from *Death & Beyond* by James N. Watkins (Carol Stream, IL: Tyndale House Publishers, 1993).

ISBN 978-1-4964-5149-1

Printed in China

27	26	25	24	23	22	21
7	6	5	4	3	2	1

To my one-hundred-year-young aunt,
Mildred Watkins Cooper.
You inspired this book!

CONTENTS

FOREWORD

As I approached my eighty-fifth birthday, I told several friends, "It's time to retire."

They laughed. Even those who were long retired.

But I knew. I'd lost my enthusiasm, and my work no longer excited me. I began asking God, "What should I do with the rest of my life?" I didn't want to just fill time; I wanted to enjoy myself with meaningful and helpful challenges.

I'd already served as a missionary, a pastor, and a professional ghostwriter; I had traveled to six continents and written more than one hundred books; and I wasn't concerned about running out of money before I died. What was there for an old guy like me to do so I could feel useful and not just take up space on earth?

For one year I heard no answer. Then two things happened in answer to that persistent prayer. First, I volunteered to serve Communion as an ordained minister every month to shut-ins. I stepped up because I saw a need and no one else was doing it.

Second, a literary agent asked me, unsolicited, if I would mentor one of her clients. He had a fine book idea but couldn't write well enough for publication. For five months, I worked diligently with him, mostly by email. He worked hard and wrote his book, and the agent sold it.

Although it was a joyful experience, I didn't anticipate doing that again. And yet, only a few months later, a book editor asked me if I would mentor two people she felt showed promise. I agreed and marveled at their commitment and progress. That experience opened me to accept other want-to-be-published writers. That number has now grown to five, which seems enough.

I cite both examples because they enabled me to learn invaluable lessons about myself—concepts I hadn't thought of before. While engaged in those two ministries, I realized *they needed me*. I supplied something for them they couldn't do themselves. And they, in turn, gave me something. *Fulfillment. A sense of purpose.*

I hadn't realized that serving others would change *me*. I was serving others and that was reward enough. Or so I assumed.

One of my first insights was that helping wasn't something I did out of the goodness of my heart; I acknowledged that each act of kindness became part of my "repaying" God for giving me the gift of life. Meeting others' needs provided opportunities to confirm to God my gratitude for being alive.

My most simple—but profound—insight came more recently. I realized something new about myself. *I need to be needed.* Truly, I hadn't thought of that before. In responding to the needs of others, I was also responding to Cec Murphey's needs.

Since gaining that insight, every morning as I pray for the shut-ins and my protégé writers by name, I feel blessed by God. *I'm needed.* I'm an instrument in God's hands. By his grace, I can help others improve their lives, and the big payoff is that I experience greater fulfillment.

Giving has also become a powerful step in loving and caring for myself. For me to face my need was liberating, and it filled my heart with joy.

I'm still alive, healthy, and enjoying my life. I marvel that I can bless others, and what they don't know is that I'm the greater recipient of grace.

So if you're not dead, you're not done with life and God's not finished with you.

As you read my friend's book, I trust you'll find hope and humor for your aging adventure.

Cecil ("Cec") Murphey
Coauthor of the *New York Times* bestsellers
90 Minutes in Heaven and
Gifted Hands: The Ben Carson Story

Old Forks Home

INTRODUCTION

Therefore we do not lose heart. Though outwardly we are wasting away, yet inwardly we are being renewed day by day. For our light and momentary troubles are achieving for us an eternal glory that far outweighs them all. So we fix our eyes not on what is seen, but on what is unseen, since what is seen is temporary, but what is unseen is eternal.

2 CORINTHIANS 4:16-18, NIV

Hi, I'm Jim. Welcome to Agers Anonymous.

This is my brand-new support group, and I am so glad you've taken time out of your busy schedule to join me. I'm honored.

With ten thousand of us turning sixty-five each day, there's definitely a need for this group and these ten steps. (Yes, I know, most *anonymous* groups have twelve steps, but I can barely remember the three words the doctor has me recall during my annual checkup. (Actually, the three words for the cognitive test were *dog*, *book*, and *grass*, but don't ask me what I had for breakfast!)

So, I'll be sharing ten characteristics that I believe are essential for being . . .

2 ll IF YOU'RE NOT DEAD, YOU'RE NOT DONE

A Saintly, Satisfied, and Significant Senior

My basic premise is that aging is all in our heads: hair loss, diminished sight, decreased hearing, missing teeth as well as the addition of chin and ear hair! And yet, those are only what the apostle Paul calls "outward" signs. Most important is what is happening "inwardly" and not simply the side effects of our many orbits around the sun. We all know *young* octogenarians and some really *old* thirtysomethings. The difference is on what we choose to "fix our eyes."

A Tale of Two Seniors

Let me introduce you to my aunt Mildred, one hundred, a founding member of Agers Anonymous, and my friend Karl, eighty-two. (To avoid a lawsuit, that's not Karl's real name.)

Mildred lights up whatever room she enters with a mischievous smile that warns you her mind is still sharp and she's ready to deliver snarky one-liners. Years ago, when she was a stay-at-home mom, she volunteered as a teacher's aide, staying on even after her own three daughters retired from teaching. She finally gave up the classroom at ninety years old when she became legally blind. And although she can't see the board, she loves games and has us all laughing whenever we get together for game night.

I asked her the secret to her delightful demeanor. "Well, every morning, I get myself out of bed and force myself to do things. But by 7 p.m., I'm exhausted, so I just lie in bed and thank God for all my blessings."

Karl retired from factory work at sixty-five, but had been active in building his own house, teaching Sunday school, and serving as lay leader in his church. He also did volunteer work, building ramps and remodeling living space for people with physical limitations. He enjoyed having his grandchildren spend a week with him in the summer.

But as Karl's physical health declined, so did his mental health. Now, living in an assisted-living facility, he had stopped going to the dining room, and eventually ate his meals alone in his room. Karl's one source of joy was receiving his church's prayer list and praying through it fervently. But even that took second place to obsessing about his health. He often called me with graphic details of his bowel movements and prostate issues.

Whenever I visited I would tell him, "If you wake up, God has something meaningful for you to do that day. If you're not dead, you're not done."

You're Not Done

That's the premise of this book of encouraging Scriptures and inspiring quotations, as well as practical ways to make a difference, no matter what your physical or mental limitations.

Despite how we may be wasting away, we are not done. And not to brag, but I've had four surgeries in three hospitals in just two months, battled cancer and debilitating radiation treatments, broken a few bones, am legally blind in my left eye, have arthritis that makes turning my neck sound like the snap-crackle-pop of a bowl of Rice Krispies, struggle with clinical depression, and . . . uh . . . oh yeah . . . struggle with memory issues. So I'm not insensitive to what you may be facing.

But I believe God wants to renew us spiritually and empower us so we may "still bear fruit in old age, [and] stay fresh and green" (Psalm 92:14, NIV). I love it! We can be old and gnarled like an ancient vine, but still be full of life and producing lush, green leaves and wine-worthy grapes.

We don't have to turn bitter like short-story author and playwright Dorothy Park apparently became in old age: "Don't feel bad when I die; I've been dead a long time."[1]

So join me in the journey of being old, yet still alive and being renewed day by day. Aging really is all in your head. Your thinking and attitudes will determine your age much more accurately than the number of candles on your birthday cake. Spend your time meditating on those things that are unseen and eternal, and incorporating the ten characteristics of Agers Anonymous into your daily living.

At my age . . . I get my daily paper, look at the obituaries page, and if I'm not there, I carry on as usual.
PATRICK MOORE

AGERS ANONYMOUS

PART I
ACCEPTANCE

We admitted we were powerless over aches and pains, weaknesses, memory issues, and all the other consequences of aging that had become unmanageable.

I am certain that God,
who began the good work within you,
will continue his work until it is finally finished
on the day when Christ Jesus returns.

PHILIPPIANS 1:6

Methuselah and his offspring

1

AGERS ANONYMOUS

I will be your God throughout your lifetime—until your hair
is white with age. I made you, and I will care for you.
I will carry you along and save you.

ISAIAH 46:4

As I wrote earlier, with ten thousand men and women turning sixty-five each day, I believe there's a need for "Agers
Anonymous." Welcome to our first meeting! Here are my
ten steps that I believe are essential in being a satisfied,
significant, and saintly senior:

1. **Acceptance** of aches, pains, and all the other
   unmanageable consequences of aging

I remember the day in great detail. A warm, sunny day
in July, slight breeze from the north and a stainless-steel pro-
pane grill that our son needed moved from the second-story
deck to the patio beneath it.

"Hey, Dad, can you help me move this grill?"

"Sure."

Mustering up my machismo, I grabbed one end and . . . nothing. I strained every muscle as Paul easily lifted the other end. I tried again and again . . . nothing. And the final blow . . . his petite wife grabbed my end and easily helped him carry the grill down the stairs.

I vividly remember a desire to run and hide and have a good cry. I was old . . . and weak. My son's childhood hero had met his kryptonite!

So the very first step for all of us is to bravely confront reality that the traumatic changes of aging affect us—physically, mentally, socially, and even spiritually. Only then can we live fully one day at a time in the remaining steps:

2. **Anticipation** of a brighter future as we live fully in the present

3. **Courage** to face each new day without fear

4. **Curiosity** to keep exploring this amazing world and stay young by learning new things

5. **Faith, hope, and love** from Bible study, prayer, and fellowship with God and others

6. **Forgiveness** by making amends with anyone we have a grudge against or have called "an old goat"

7. **Gratitude** for God's love and care, replacing all our wrong attitudes toward aging

8. **Joy** through asking God to swap our complaints with things that help us experience *his* joy

9. **Optimism** by deliberately choosing positive thoughts based on God's "good, pleasing and perfect will"[2]

10. **Significance** realized by being energized with God's power and living out these ten steps daily

Thanks again for coming to the meeting.

> *God grant me the serenity*
> *to accept the things I cannot change;*
> *the courage to change the things I can;*
> *and the willingness not to whine about them.*

To Do

Choose one step to work on this week. Continue working on a new step each week. Visit agersanonymous.com for regular postings of hope and humor on aging.

"Well, first, let me give you
the good news."

2

TO AVOID AGING, DIE YOUNG

My health may fail, and my spirit may grow weak,
but God remains the strength of my heart; he is mine forever.

PSALM 73:26

The odometer on my 1952 Model Watkins just turned over to sixty-nine!

It shows a lot of wear and tear: balding tires, dented fenders, and a bit of body corrosion—not to mention issues with clogged fuel lines, high engine pressure, and some major body work (four trips to three repair shops in just two months in 1991) plus, in 2008, forty-two days up on the rack at an auto specialist to give this rattletrap new life.

Theories of why we fall apart fall into two parts: wear and tear and planned obsolescence.

Wear and Tear

Our cells busily reproduce themselves throughout our lifetime. During all this multiplying and dividing of protein, our DNA (genetic blueprint) occasionally makes a mistake. Scientists speculate that exposure to toxins, chemicals, and ultraviolet light breaks, twists, or scrambles these genetic codes. Cells begin to break down and our bodies begin to show signs of aging: loss of muscle strength and lung capacity as well as decreasing heart and kidney effectiveness.

Another cause of wear and tear may be blood sugar called glucose. High levels can cause protein cells to stick together into a gooey mess, clouding our eyes, clogging arteries, gumming up kidney functions, and making breathing difficult.

Not only do we get sticky and gooey, we also rust with age! Oxygen and "free radicals" allegedly cause protein to "rust" much the same way rain and snow cause a car to fall apart. Scientists believe these molecular muggers can cause arthritis, diabetes, hardening of the arteries, heart and kidney failure, lung disease, and cancer.[3]

Planned Obsolescence

Vehicles and humans begin to self-destruct once the warranty expires. Life spans have been remarkably consistent since Moses wrote, "Seventy years are given to us! Some even live to eighty" (Psalm 90:10). Today in North America, men can expect to live until 76, women to 81 years.[4]

Researchers claim that the longest possible lifetime is between 115 and 120. But that's no new discovery either. After incredibly long life spans prior to the Flood, God declared, "My Spirit will not put up with humans for such a long time, for they are only mortal flesh. In the future, their normal lifespan will be no more than 120 years" (Genesis 6:3). Sure enough, "Moses was 120 years old when he died" (Deuteronomy 34:7).

Increasing Your Years

We can increase our life expectancy with all the usual remedies: eat right, exercise, don't smoke or use illegal drugs. But despite all that, physical life is still terminal. Admit it.

But here's the good news—finally!

"Though outwardly we are wasting away, yet inwardly we are being renewed day by day" (2 Corinthians 4:16, NIV).

Our spirit will live forever! As our physical bodies deteriorate, God is enlivening our spiritual being day by day. You're not getting older, you're getting better!

I intend to live forever. So far, so good.
STEVEN WRIGHT

To Do

Do something today to improve your physical or spiritual life.
(Consult your doctor before attempting mixed martial arts, ultramarathons, or running with the bulls.)

"He calls the couch
his 'recharging station.'"

3

I'M NOT NAPPING, I'M RECHARGING

Jesus said, "Come to me, all of you who are weary and carry heavy burdens, and I will give you rest."

MATTHEW 11:28

Our phones, laptops, and digital cameras all need recharging. And so do human brains. And not just eight hours at a time. Scientists are discovering that "power naps" reboot our brains and offer remarkable results.

In *Take a Nap! Change Your Life*, Dr. Sara Mednick at the University of California writes, "You can get incredible benefits from fifteen to twenty minutes of napping. You reset the system and get a burst of alertness and increased motor performance."[5] But wait, there's more!

A study of 23,681 men and women found that those who napped three times per week had a 37 percent lower risk of dying from heart disease.[6] Research has also shown that daytime naps can boost creativity, reduce stress, enhance one's sex life, aid in weight loss, brighten your mood, boost memory, and improve perception, stamina, motor skills, and accuracy.[7]

And if you're a morning person, journalist Pete Hamill writes, "The replenishing thing that comes with a nap [is] you end up with two mornings in a day."[8]

Professor Leon Lack from Flinders University in Australia notes that "Ten to fifteen minutes of sleep seems to be the optimum period in terms of improving mental operations, performance, reaction times and subjective feelings of alertness."[9]

However, Dr. Mednick writes, "For cognitive memory processing, however, a sixty-minute nap may do more good [as it] helps with remembering facts, places, and faces. The downside: some grogginess upon waking. Finally, the ninety-minute nap will likely involve a full cycle of sleep, which aids creativity and emotional and procedural memory."[10]

The Bible also reveals the power of naps.

Elijah was "a man of God" (2 Kings 1:12) who "lay down and slept under the broom tree" (1 Kings 19:5) and then got up to eat and was strengthened. As someone has commented, "Sometimes you just need a nap and a snack."[11]

But the greatest example is Jesus himself in Matthew 8. After a busy chapter of healing the Roman officer's servant and Peter's mother-in-law, a late night of casting out demons and healing all the sick brought to him, a morning of teaching and confronting the teachers of the Law, Jesus took a nap on the boat. It apparently was short-lived; his disciples woke him up as a violent storm came up. He commanded the wind and waves to be still, and then—I'm guessing—he shook his head at the disciples' lack of faith and went back to finish his nap.

So with the encouragement of Elijah, Jesus, and modern research, enjoy a daily nap for better physical and mental health.

I never drink coffee at lunch,
I find it keeps me awake for the afternoon.
PRESIDENT RONALD REAGAN

To Do

Take a nap!

"Yay—I just won a Grammy!"

4

BEAUTY IS BUT SKIN-DEEP, UGLY TO THE BONE

Don't be concerned about the outward beauty of fancy hairstyles, expensive jewelry, or beautiful clothes. You should clothe yourselves instead with the beauty that comes from within, the unfading beauty of a gentle and quiet spirit, which is so precious to God.

1 PETER 3:3-4

According to my highly unscientific study in front of the bathroom mirror, the earth's gravitational force has been steadily increasing since I turned forty! It's pulling my face downward to collect under my chin. Other parts are also heading south. If not for my belt, my chest would be around my ankles! And it's been forty years since someone called me "Slim Jim." I *am* still "skinny," but only in the sense I have a *lot* of skin!

But novelist Dorothy West writes in *The Wedding*, "Beauty is but skin deep, ugly to the bone. And when beauty fades away, ugly claims its own."[12]

Unfortunately, our modern culture's concept of beauty is only skin deep, as evidenced by all the anti-aging products designed to deny nature's ongoing process. Witty writer

Dorothy Parker noted, "Time may be a great healer, but it's a lousy beautician."[13]

That's why I love Margery Williams's classic children's book *The Velveteen Rabbit*. And like all great children's books, it offers wisdom to older adults as well. Such is the case of her wonderful observation that being real is the secret to being beautiful:

> "Real isn't how you are made," said the Skin Horse. "It's a thing that happens to you. When a child loves you for a long, long time, not just to play with, but *really* loves you, then you become Real."
>
> "Does it hurt?" asked the Rabbit.
>
> "Sometimes," said the Skin Horse, for he was always truthful. "When you are Real you don't mind being hurt."
>
> "Does it happen all at once, like being wound up," he asked, "or bit by bit?"
>
> "It doesn't happen all at once," said the Skin Horse. "You become. It takes a long time. That's why it doesn't happen often to people who break easily, or have sharp edges, or who have to be carefully kept. Generally, by the time you are Real, most of your hair has been loved off, and your eyes drop out and you get loose in the joints and very shabby. But these things don't matter at all, because once you are Real you can't be ugly, except to people who don't understand."[14]

I'm afraid *The Velveteen Rabbit* wasn't required reading for the generation that has grown up with the unreality of PhotoShop, Instagram, and Snapchat filters, as well as carefully staged selfies. The images are as fake as urban legends and are spreading like COVID across social networks.

Yep, my hair is thinning, I'm legally blind in my left eye, and I do look a bit shabby, but I found a card on the lectern where I was speaking at a conference. I was shocked to read in the thank-you card, "We can see Jesus in you, Jim." That's what I want people to see—and apparently, every once in a while, I get it right.

May you radiate the "unfading beauty"—or rugged good looks—"of a gentle and quiet spirit, which is so precious to God."

Beautiful young people are accidents of nature,
but beautiful old people are works of art.
ELEANOR ROOSEVELT

To Do

Develop a daily beauty routine—
for the inside.

"How long has it been since you went
wee wee wee all the way home?"

5
GRIN AND BARE IT

We can't escape the constant humiliation;
shame is written across our faces.

PSALM 44:15

I'm sure one of the reams of forms we fill out upon entering the hospital reads:

Release of Modesty

Patient, upon entering hospital, surgical center, or any healthcare facility, at the discretion of any and all authorized medical staff, shall relinquish all modesty, including, but not limited to, bashfulness, decorum, dignity, discretion, embarrassment, privacy, propriety, and/or sense of shame or shyness.

I had been someone who always locked the bathroom door—even when I was home alone. And so when I went in to have my reproductive plumbing lines shut off, I realized that I had indeed signed away all rights to my personal space.

23

I won't go into details, but let's just say the pre-op was embarrassing, but nothing compared to post-op. Every ten minutes a young female nurse would stroll in, throw back the covers, and check my incisions. File this under "Constant humiliation; shame written across my face."

I felt all dignity and inhibition draining slowly from my entire being. It finally got to the point that when she entered the room, I threw back the covers like some deviant's trench coat. Since then I've endured colonoscopies, prostate cancer biopsies, and a stubborn kidney stone that required three surgeries in three hospitals over two months to pry it loose. I thought I had reached the height of humiliation. But oh no!

My mother had problems with circulation in her legs, so she had at least three implants of titanium stents inserted in her femoral arteries. Amazingly, it was an outpatient surgery, but it required someone at home to inspect the point of entry in the groin every two hours. Again, no details, but let's just say I saw things I hadn't seen since Mom gave birth to me. We both tried to be nonchalant about it, but it was truly traumatic for both of us. (I should probably talk to a therapist!) Gradually, we became more comfortable as the years passed, getting to the point where I could help with toileting without turning completely red-faced.

Maybe you are at that point where catheters, adult diapers, and suppositories are a part of your daily life. I'm sure you can relate to the apostle Paul when he writes about how the "bodies we have now embarrass us" (1 Corinthians 15:43, TLB).

I'm not sure I have any advice on how to handle these humiliations except to express thanks to medical staff and brave family members who love you enough to take on these tasks that are uncomfortable for both of you.

And hang on to the psalmist's promise as he writes, "My health may fail, and my spirit may grow weak, but God remains the strength of my heart; he is mine forever" (Psalm 73:26). But most of all, we need to realize that we are not our bodies. We are an everlasting soul imprisoned in a temporary—and embarrassing—body.

The embarrassment of a situation can, once you are over it, be the funniest time in your life. And I suppose a lot of my comedy comes from painful moments or experiences in life, and you just flip them on their head.

MIRANDA HART

To Do

Write a thank-you note to your medical staff or loved ones for caring for your personal needs.

"Hi, I'm looking for a new church.
One with wealthy widowers."

6

"ONE" IS *NOT* THE LONELIEST NUMBER

I will not abandon you as orphans—I will come to you. . . .
When I am raised to life again, you will know that I am
in my Father, and you are in me, and I am in you.

JOHN 14:18, 20

Three Dog Night took the song "One" to number five on the charts in 1969.[15] It's best known for its claim that "one is the loneliest number."

It does feel excruciatingly lonely when a spouse, child, relative, best friend, or other loved one dies.

That's because grief is an emotion of loss. Perhaps you have also felt that emotion when you left the home in which you raised your family to move into assisted living or even when your new abode stopped celebrating "Taco Tuesday" due to the rash of GI problems among the residents. There's a feeling of separation and loss.

Grief and love are two very similar emotions—if you're capable of love, you are capable of grief. Only a person who never loves never grieves. When you love someone, you feel a oneness and fulfillment with that person. But you also open

27

yourself up to the possibility for grief—when he or she breaks up with you, moves away, or dies. The relationship is over and that strong emotion of love mutates like some hideous sci-fi monster into equally strong grief.

So love is *both* the loneliest number and the most fulfilling number.

Jesus in his final lesson to his disciples teaches, "Just believe that I am in the Father and the Father is in me. . . . And you are in me, and I am in you" (John 14:11, 20). We experience that holy oneness between God the Father, God the Son, and us his children!

Paul later writes that marriage creates "one flesh" that symbolizes an even greater oneness: "This is a great mystery, but it is an illustration of the way Christ and the church are one" (Ephesians 5:32).

The apostle goes on about this wonderful oneness:

"But the person who is joined to the Lord is one spirit with him" (1 Corinthians 6:17).

"Don't you realize that all of you together are the temple of God and that the Spirit of God lives in you?" (1 Corinthians 3:16). This verse celebrates the unity we have not only with God, but with all his children as well.

For the non-Christian, yes, one is the loneliest number. (And the American rock band also notes that two can be just as bad as one.) Without the wonderful oneness of union with the Holy Trinity, any and all other relationships can be lonely.

Take heart, friends. While you may have suffered loss of a spouse, of family members, of lifelong friends, or of your home or health, you are never ever alone. Just as the Father, Son, and Spirit are one, you are one with the Trinity! And that's the best number that you'll ever do!

One is a whole number.

JNW

To Do

Meditate today on the wonderful oneness you have with God and his people. (It may take more than one day.)

7

GOOD GRIEF

*[Jesus] was despised and rejected—a man of sorrows,
acquainted with deepest grief.*

ISAIAH 53:3

I am so grateful that Jesus—the Son of Man—can relate to our human emotions! He "understands our weaknesses, for he faced all of the same testings we do" (Hebrews 4:15). When his cousin, John the Baptist, was beheaded by King Herod, Jesus went away by himself to grieve. At the tomb of his friend Lazarus, "Jesus wept" (John 11:35). The all-powerful Son of God knew loss.

We talked in the last chapter how grief is the opposite of love. Jamie Anderson perfectly describes the connection: "Grief, I've learned, is really just love. It's all the love you want to give, but cannot. All that unspent love gathers up in the corners of your eyes, the lump in your throat, and in that hollow part of your chest. Grief is just love with no place to go."[16]

We all experience loss and grieve in our own way, so please underline and highlight this: Never, ever say, "I totally understand." For instance, we may have both lost a cousin, but there are multiple differences between my loss and yours. Things you don't understand or know. What kind of relationship did we have? Were we close or did we see each other only at Christmas? What were the last words spoken? Were they loving, harsh, or worse, indifferent? What kinds of questions, thoughts, and feelings are churning in my mind? What is my concept of death? Or life after death?

You honestly don't understand. And neither do I completely understand your loss. But I can help by sharing how I completely fell apart at my cousin's brutal battle and untimely death to ALS. And in that way, I'm giving you freedom to share your grief. So I can't say I understand the grief you may be feeling.

For instance, a friend lost her son to a random shooting. I had no idea what to say, but I did sense the Spirit helping me: "I can't imagine what you're feeling, but I do know Someone who does. He lost his only Son to a torturous murder, so the Father understands the pain you're feeling." She expressed how helpful that was to her in her grief.

God the Father, the Son, and the Spirit understand. A parent who was hurting from the five-year absence of his prodigal told me this story. "One night, I was so missing my son when it struck me that God the Father has billions of prodigals.

I suddenly felt so sorry for him that I began sobbing for the pain he must be feeling. At that point I never felt closer to God—in our joint pain. He understood me—and I understood him!"

While I was interviewing people suffering grief for *Death & Beyond*, a fifteen-year-old provided a wise observation. He described his older sister's death as losing an arm. "Eventually the pain goes away, but you will always miss your arm. You can make adjustments and compensate for it, but you still have just one arm."

Yes, you may be missing the most important person or thing in your life, but please be assured, God understands. And Scripture promises, "The LORD is close to the brokenhearted; he rescues those whose spirits are crushed" (Psalm 34:18).

While our loved one is in a better place . . . we are not!

JNW

To Do

Acknowledge that you are not "in a better place," and allow yourself permission to grieve in this worst place. Allow God to understand and comfort you.

"They said my Song of Solomon
message was rated PG-13."

8

FIFTY SHADES OF GRAY HAIR

Kiss me and kiss me again,
for your love is sweeter than wine.

SONG OF SONGS 1:2

Let me begin by emphatically stating *God is pro-sex!* Need proof?

1. When God created light, the earth, and sky along with the living creatures, at the end of each day he proclaimed them "good." But it was not until God created humans, male and female, that he triumphantly deemed it "very good!" (Genesis 1:31). In other words, "I can't do any better than that. I'm taking tomorrow off!"

2. An entire Bible book, the Song of Songs, is devoted to explicit sexuality. Need proof?

   Your navel is perfectly formed
   like a goblet filled with mixed wine.

> Between your thighs lies a mound of wheat
>   bordered with lilies.
> Your breasts are like two fawns,
>   twin fawns of a gazelle.

SONG OF SONGS 7:2-3

3. And Paul claimed sexual intercourse is a symbol of the kind of intimacy Christ wants to have with the church—his bride: "As the Scriptures say, 'A man leaves his father and mother and is joined to his wife, and the two are united into one.' This is a great mystery, but it is an illustration of the way Christ and the church are one" (Ephesians 5:31-32). So don't worry about there being no earthly sex in heaven. Heavenly reality is always infinitely better than the earthly symbol. Wow!

Sex Is Better after Sixty

When *Fifty Shades of Grey* became a national bestseller and then a blockbuster movie with young, virile actors playing the kinky, sexy lovers, I wrote a snarky piece in my newspaper column: "Fifty Shades of Beige." I made the point that young and free sex is nothing compared to committed senior citizen sex. I quoted Dr. Paul Pearsall who argued, "Super sex requires super love, a love that is possible only in a relationship that lasts."[17]

And according to WebMD.com, researchers have found that "many mature couples have better love lives than they did in their more youthful days. There are lots of reasons for this. They have deeper intimacy with partners, fewer distractions, no pregnancy concerns, and just plain more time to get busy. Plus, they have much more know-how and done-that than those young things on TV."[18]

Boom! I had science on my side when I made the claim that great sex requires just as much practice as becoming a skilled pianist. While young couples are plinking out sexual "Chopsticks," their grandparents are dancing on the keys with Chopin's Étude Opus 10, Number 4.

The Challenges of Sex over Sixty

Yes, sexual activity gets better and more meaningful with age, but as we acknowledged in chapter 1, our bodies are changing.

For women, changes include the vagina shortening and narrowing, becoming thinner and drier with age. Menopause brings a plunge in estrogen and androgen, which may result in lower interest in sex.

For men, a decrease in testosterone and estrogen occurs about the same time. Lower levels of these hormones as well as collapsing blood vessels can lead to erectile disfunction. Diabetes can damage nerves and blood vessels, causing ED.

I'm not a doctor. I don't even play one on TV. But your

primary care doctor has effective solutions for each issue. And you will find a licensed therapist helpful in addressing emotional issues causing problems in your sex life.

But I am encouraged by the words of the three-times Masters golf champion from the 1940s and 50s:

> *Golf and sex are about the only things*
> *you can enjoy without being good at them.*
> JIMMY DEMARET

To Do

Use your imagination!

PART II

ANTICIPATION

Made a decision to no longer
live in the past, but to live
fully in the present as we
anticipated a brighter future.

Don't long for "the good old days."
This is not wise.

ECCLESIASTES 7:10

Grampoline

9

PUTTING THE BOOM BACK IN "BABY BOOMER"

As you serve the Lord, work hard and don't be lazy.
Be excited about serving him!

ROMANS 12:11, ERV

Nothing is more disappointing than this: A seven-year-old boy finds a stash of M-80s from a previous Fourth of July. His heart is pounding as he lights the fuse of the powerful firecracker, runs for cover, and then plugs his ears bracing for the deafening explosion. Instead, there's a *pfff* instead of *BOOM*! The powder in the explosives became moist over the years.

Sometimes we all feel like a wet firecracker. As my grandmother used to say, "I'm too pooped to pop."

Cheery chapter 1 explained why our physical bodies lose their boom, but God's Word is clear we don't have to lose explosive excitement in our emotions and spirits.

The Greek word Paul uses for this excitement in today's verse is *zeō*. Joseph Henry Thayer's *Greek-English Lexicon of the New Testament* defines the word as literally "to boil with heat." (Wow! Now that's a "hot flash"!) He notes that it's used metaphorically in the original language as "boiling anger, love, zeal, for what is good or bad, etc."

First, exhilaration doesn't come from espresso, dark chocolate, or any other external stimulant. It comes from the Spirit.

Christ promises us the Spirit will be God's presence on earth (John 16:7) and will convict us of our need for God (John 16:8). For believers, he lives within us (John 14:16-17), teaches us God's truth (John 14:26), assures us that we are God's children (Romans 8:16), prays on our behalf (Romans 8:26), and transforms obedient believers into Christlike people (Romans 8:9-11).

But wait, there's more! The Holy Spirit comes to bring us power. The Greek word for power throughout the New Testament is *dunamis*, from which we get the word *dynamite*. (A whole ammo box of M-80s.) Here are just a few verses in Scripture that mention the power dwelling within us through the Spirit.

> He gives power to the weak
>   and strength to the powerless.
>
> ISAIAH 40:29

> It is not by force nor by strength, but by my Spirit,
> says the LORD of Heaven's Armies.
>
> ZECHARIAH 4:6

The Kingdom of God is not just a lot of talk;
it is living by God's power.

1 CORINTHIANS 4:20

The Holy Spirit produces this kind of fruit in our
lives: love, joy, peace, patience, kindness, goodness,
faithfulness, gentleness, and self-control.

GALATIANS 5:22-23

Notice that this power doesn't come *upon* us, but God the
Spirit lives *inside* us, filling us with power, enthusiasm, zeal,
and boiling-hot passion to live for him. *BOOM!*

Choose thoughts that give you the emotions
of being alive and excited about life.

BRYANT McGILL

To Do

If you have never asked the
Holy Spirit to fill you with his power,
please do that today.
(Here's a helpful post:
www.jameswatkins.com/spirit)

"I'm sorry, sir. I thought you were trying to check in early. You certainly don't act 99!"

10

I WANT TO DIE VERY YOUNG AT A VERY OLD AGE

Even in old age they will still produce fruit;
they will remain vital and green.

PSALM 92:14

On my fiftieth birthday, I wrote the following for my weekly newspaper column:

> While I'm still in reasonably sound mind and body, I have in my wrinkled right hand, direct from my home office in Corn Borer, Indiana, today's top ten wishes for my fiftieth birthday.

10. **I will not obsess about my cholesterol level, the cost of prescriptions, or the condition of my colon.** Also off-limits during the Early Bird dinner hour at Denny's: Social Security rip-offs, government corruption, and "that horrible noise they call modern music."

45

9. **I will eat right and exercise so I can be around for fifty more birthdays with grandkids, great-grandkids, great-great . . .**

8. **I will not complain about the younger generation.** After all, *my* generation has given the world international dictators, crazy cult leaders, blood-thirsty terrorists, and polyester leisure suits!

7. **I will not long for "the good old days."** What was "good" about polio, smallpox, the Cold War with nuclear attack drills in school, racial segregation and gender discrimination, JFK and RFK and MLK's assassinations . . . ? Well, you get the idea.

6. **When I have the chance, I hope I'll dance.** I always close the curtains so neighbors don't call 911 for man having seizure.

5. **I will not let my brain go to seed.** I will continue to learn new things through people, print, and pixels as long as I have eyes to read or ears to hear.

4. **I will hold on tight to my dreams and ideals.** Poet Samuel Ullman wrote, "Years may wrinkle the skin, but to give up enthusiasm wrinkles the soul."[19]

3. **I won't buy into Madison Avenue's, Wall Street's, or even Main Street's definition of "success."** I love what Bessie Anderson Stanley wrote about success.

To laugh often and much; To win the respect of intelligent people and the affection of children; To earn the appreciation of honest critics and endure the betrayal of false friends; To appreciate beauty, to find the best in others; To leave the world a bit better, whether by a healthy child, a garden patch, or a redeemed social condition; To know even one life has breathed easier because you lived. This is to have succeeded.[20]

2. **When I meet my final deadline, I want to hear my Editor say, "Enter in, thou good and faithful servant."** And my number one goal:

1. **I want to be alive when I die.** Rabbi Harold Kushner wrote, "If a person lives and dies and no one notices, if the world continues as it was, was that person ever really alive?"[21]

> *We don't stop playing because we grow old.*
> *We grow old because we stop playing.*
> GEORGE BERNARD SHAW

To Do

Take one of the top ten and make that your goal for today.

"Just trying to reach
my peak potential."

11

OVER THE HILL . . .
ONTO THE MOUNTAINTOP

God arms me with strength, and he makes my way perfect.
He makes me as surefooted as a deer,
enabling me to stand on mountain heights.

PSALM 18:32-33

In Scripture, forty is a frightening number! The Flood lasted forty days and nights. Goliath taunted the Israelites for forty days. Moses, running from the law, hid out in the desert for forty years. The rebellious Israelites wandered in the desert for forty years. Jesus was tempted in the desert for forty days. And forty lashes was one of the punishments handed down by the Sanhedrin.

No wonder turning forty is so traumatic!

One of my professors told us young, idealistic—and just a bit egotistical and naive—ministerial students, "Not only does life begin at forty, but everything you do before is just practice for what you will accomplish in the last forty years."

That was incredibly insulting for us young bucks and does who were planning to change the world the moment we graduated. But here's what I've learned: *When you're "over the hill," it's onto the mountaintop!*

That's not original. I'm borrowing it from my friend Louise L. Looney, a delightful woman twenty years my elder, who asked me to help her write the book *Over the Hill . . . Onto the Mountaintop*. It's filled with wit and wisdom for the latter forty-plus years. She writes:

> The world announces we've reached a time when we are "over the hill." That should imply we can coast for the rest of the way, right? No! God didn't give any of us permission to lean back and take it easy. And don't count on Him giving us a little push to slide downhill for the rest of the way home. Learn, live and laugh, we're on our way! Over the hill . . . and onto the mountaintop![22]

Looking back, I realize my professor and Louise were absolutely right. Everything I did before forty was simply trial and error for what I'm doing now. All those years of speaking to youth groups, writing weekly devotionals for my youth group, working as editorial director at a Christian publishing house, and trying to be a good husband and dad paved the way for my writing and speaking today.

I was forty when my first book was published by a major publisher. (Thanks, Tyndale House.) And I was forty when

I was confronted by Thomas à Kempis's convicting words in *The Imitation of Christ*: "If you wish to learn and appreciate something worthwhile, then love to be unknown and considered as nothing." Ouch! I was forty-eight when I started regularly speaking overseas.

To be totally honest, top-of-the-hill Jim was kind of a selfish, arrogant jerk. I like onto-the-mountaintop Jim much better. And I hope my family, friends, readers, and listeners like him better now, thirty years further along up the mountainside.

And so each day, I try to take a few more steps up the mountain by studying my Bible; praying for direction, strength, and stamina; and learning new things about God, our world, and myself.

I want to keep climbing until one day, God will say to me, as he did to Moses, "Present yourself to me on the top of the mountain" (Exodus 34:2).

Getting old is like climbing a mountain.
You get a little out of breath, but the view is much better.

INGRID BERGMAN

To Do

Take one step higher up God's mountain.

"Your sermons always warm
my heart. Or maybe it's just gas."

12

ACID REFLUX AND FIRE IN THE BELLY

[The LORD's] word burns in my heart like a fire. It's like a fire in my bones! I am worn out trying to hold it in! I can't do it!

JEREMIAH 20:9

If you have suffered from acid reflux, you know all about "fire in the belly." You knew you shouldn't have eaten that second bowl of "Five-Alarm" chili. You've overdosed on Tums and now are lying in bed trying to ignore the flames shooting from your stomach up through your esophagus. You fear what's coming—or more accurately—what's coming *up*. There is going to be a call to action!

It's the same with fire in the belly. The prophet Jeremiah describes his passion to share the Lord's word as heartburn that he can't hold in. He, too, needs to act or there's going to be a genuine, documented case of human spontaneous combustion!

What passions burn in your heart? What fire keeps you awake nights? Without that burning that demands release, we become cold, with no desire to do anything.

Paul prays for Timothy that he will "stir up" the original passion he felt when the elder anointed and appointed him to pastor the church in Ephesus (2 Timothy 1:6-7, KJV).

What are some things you need to stir up? What gave you a sense of purpose when you were younger? What passions that have grown cold need to be stirred into flame again?

I loved writing and performing original songs. I led worship at my wife's church for ten years. But now, that passion has grown cold. I haven't performed in years.

Likewise, my wife and I traveled the United States in a motor home performing "Kids Krusades," which were a sanctified *Sesame Street* with music, puppets, and magic. Again, "The Platypus Players" have not performed for years.

Sometimes these passions are for only a season—a fruitful and productive season, but only a season. But what passions go way, way back? What gave you a sense of purpose even as a child?

My love for writing began in my early childhood when I would buy hardcover journals to write my stories and nonfiction works. That was followed by writing a play to be performed at my elementary school, serving as an editor of the high school paper, writing for my denomination's youth department, and then serving as editorial director of its publishing house. I've been in publishing and public speaking since second grade. And the joy of writing is that it requires no physical strength, so I've finished two books recovering from surgery with an ice pack down my pants and served as communications pastor at a megachurch while totally exhausted from undergoing radiation treatments. (Cancer-free since 2008!)

The privilege of sharing with the world insights I sense God has given me is what gets me pumped in the morning. It's a better form of that same kind of burning urgency that gets me out of bed and racing to the bathroom with acid reflux.

So, what is a passion you could rekindle to make a meaningful difference in this world? Writing? (Notes of encouragement count and are so appreciated.) Painting? Praying for family, friends, those in ministry? (So very important!) Tutoring or mentoring a skill you taught before retirement? Volunteering at a local ministry? There are people waiting to receive your gift.

None are so old as those who have outlived enthusiasm.
HENRY DAVID THOREAU

To Do

Rekindle a passion that gave you a sense of purpose and significance.

"The last time I had a complete physical, I had 33 percent more of my original body parts."

13
A BODY TO DIE FOR

While we live in these earthly bodies, we groan and sigh,
but it's not that we want to die and get rid of these bodies
that clothe us. Rather, we want to put on our new bodies
so that these dying bodies will be swallowed up by life.

2 CORINTHIANS 5:4

During my twenties, I was actually a hair model. Yep, my hair-stylist would take me to local beautician shows to demonstrate his unique style on my thick, long, glorious hair. (It *was* the 70s!) By thirty, my hair was turning gray, and at fifty it started turning loose. Now the only modeling I do is "Before" pictures.

The good news is that our bodies are only temporary. The Bible promises a brand-new body! Here are some clues as to what our "After" body is going to be.

Our heavenly body will be like Christ's resurrected body. It was apparently different in appearance so his closest friends didn't immediately recognize him, but they did recognize his voice and personality. Some have suggested that we will know others in heaven by their unique characteristics, rather than by their appearance (1 Corinthians 13:12).

Christ's resurrected body wasn't a ghostly form—it could

be touched and could eat a meal (Luke 24:38-43). In fact, Revelation 19:7-9 reveals that we'll do a lot of eating in heaven. (Now that *will* be heaven: a seven-year feast and we won't gain a pound!) Christ's new body could also walk through solid doors (John 20:19) and float through the sky (Acts 1:9). Is that cool or what?

It may be that our heavenly bodies are multidimensional. Currently, most people are bound by a three-dimensional prison of height, width, and depth. Imagine if we all lived in a two-dimensional world of only height and width. We would be bound to this flat world just as these ink spots are bound to this flat page. If someone arrived from a three-dimensional universe—a place that included depth—they would seem to have remarkable powers. By jumping into the air they would seem to have disappeared, because all we know is this flat two-dimensional plane to which we're confined.

These new bodies may be the "mansions" that Jesus promises: "There is more than enough room in my Father's home. If this were not so, would I have told you that I am going to prepare a place for you? When everything is ready, I will come and get you, so that you will always be with me where I am" (John 14:2-3).

The Bible refers to these "homes" as new bodies:

For we know that when this earthly tent we live in is taken down (that is, when we die and leave this earthly body), we will have a house in heaven, an eternal body made for us by God himself and not by human hands. We grow weary in our present bodies, and we long to put on our heavenly bodies like new clothing. For we will put on heavenly bodies; we will not be spirits without bodies.

2 CORINTHIANS 5:1-3

> *"I finally have the smoking-hot body*
> *I have always wanted."*
>
> SYBIL MARIE HICKS'S OBITUARY,
> NOTING SHE WAS CREMATED

To Do

Make a list of all your factory and replacement parts that are still working. Thank God for each one.

PART III

COURAGE

Humbly turned our aging
minds, bodies, and souls over
to the care of God and now can
fearlessly face each new day.

Be strong and courageous, and do the work. Don't be
afraid or discouraged, for the LORD God, my God,
is with you. He will not fail you or forsake you.

1 CHRONICLES 28:20

"If you don't stop with the worry warts, you're gonna croak."

14

FEAR IS INEVITABLE; WORRY IS OPTIONAL

Refuse to worry, and keep your body healthy.

ECCLESIASTES 11:10

You can't really scare those of us over sixty-five. We've survived too many wars to count, deadly race riots, numerous mass shootings, and domestic terrorist attacks, including 9/11, COVID, riding without seat belts or helmets, tetherball, and of course, the great toilet paper shortage of 2020. And many of us have survived "terminal" illnesses, heart attacks, and strokes—some numerous times.

The fact that you're over sixty-five and reading this book is a testament to your survival skills and the grace of God! We've survived the worst the world can throw at us—and we're still here! So there's a pretty good chance we'll be here tomorrow.

The world into which Jesus came offered much to fear. Leprosy, cholera, tuberculosis, smallpox, and dysentery suppressed life expectancy to the age of thirty-five.[23] That figure was the result of a 25 to 33 percent infant mortality rate with half of all children dying before age ten. The Roman head of the family decided if a newborn was allowed to live or left to die or be picked up by slave traders at the city landfill. Women were considered a man's property, with the accepted attitude, "Wives are for babies; mistresses for pleasure." And Jewish men prayed, "I thank God I am not a Gentile, a dog, or a woman." Into this culture, Jesus speaks, "Do not worry."

> I tell you not to worry about everyday life—whether you have enough food and drink, or enough clothes to wear. Isn't life more than food, and your body more than clothing? Look at the birds. They don't plant or harvest or store food in barns, for your heavenly Father feeds them. And aren't you far more valuable to him than they are? Can all your worries add a single moment to your life?
>
> And why worry about your clothing? Look at the lilies of the field and how they grow. They don't work or make their clothing, yet Solomon in all his glory was not dressed as beautifully as they are. And if God cares so wonderfully for wildflowers that are here today and thrown into the fire tomorrow, he will certainly care for you. Why do you have so little faith?
>
> So don't worry about these things, saying, 'What will we eat? What will we drink? What will we wear?' These things dominate the thoughts of unbelievers,

but your heavenly Father already knows all your needs. Seek the Kingdom of God above all else, and live righteously, and he will give you everything you need.

So don't worry about tomorrow, for tomorrow will bring its own worries. Today's trouble is enough for today.

MATTHEW 6:25-34

Fear is hardwired into our mind and body. Without fear of fire, heights, wild animals, natural disasters, disease, etc., we wouldn't have survived childhood. It's part of our God-given inborn instinct for survival.

However, worry is a choice. Will I worry about what I will eat, drink, or wear? Will I worry about tomorrow? Those needs require trust in a loving God who provides for his children.

Worry is like a rocking chair:
It gives you something to do but never gets you anywhere.
ERMA BOMBECK

To Do

Each time a worry comes to mind, replace it with a memory of how God provided for a similar concern.

"Red Bull in the
Communion cups again?"

15

DON'T GET OLDER, GET BOLDER

Be strong and courageous.

JOSHUA 1:6

Joshua had just assumed leadership of the Hebrew people after the death of Moses. They had endured forty years wandering the desert as a punishment for their rebellion, and now Moses, who had led them out of slavery in Egypt, was dead. That's a *grande*-sized challenge!

But in three different verses, God commands him, "Be strong and courageous" (Joshua 1:6), "Be strong and very courageous" (1:7), and "Be strong and courageous! Do not be afraid or discouraged. For the Lord your God is with you wherever you go" (1:9).

Are you facing such a challenge? Packing up your home to sell? Moving into assisted living or in with your family? Being told you have chronic illness? Having lost your spouse? Figuring out your new phone?

67

You may feel like these challenges compare to what Joshua and the eleven other scouts found as they explored the Promised Land. Like the ten men who gave a pessimistic report of seeing formidable giants: "Next to them we felt like grasshoppers, and that's what they thought, too!" (Numbers 13:33).

How could Joshua be strong and courageous, not afraid or discouraged?! Only one way. He believed God's promise. "For the LORD your God is with you wherever you go" (Joshua 1:9).

This is the exact same promise Jesus gave his disciples on the Sea of Galilee when "they were in serious trouble, rowing hard and struggling against the wind and waves" (Mark 6:48).

Jesus casually walked across the tops of the waves and called out, "Take courage! I am here!" (Mark 6:50).

It's the identical promise God the Father had made to Joshua. The original Greek can also be translated, "The 'I AM' is here!" Remember, I AM is the name God gives himself to Moses from the burning bush. And now Jesus is using the same title! God the Son is saying "I, God, am here."

One more thing: We often think of "brave and courageous" as involving knights battling fire-breathing dragons, a general leading his men into a fierce fight, or a superhero taking on an equally super villain. Perhaps that just sounds exhausting at your age.

But David writes, "Wait patiently for the LORD. Be brave and courageous. Yes, wait patiently for the LORD" (Psalm 27:14). He also says, "Be still in the presence of the LORD, and wait patiently for him to act" (Psalm 37:7).

Paul writes about our life-and-death battle with "evil rulers and authorities of the unseen world, against mighty powers in this dark world, and against evil spirits in the heavenly places" (Ephesians 6:12). But what are we told to do? To simply "stand" in the protective armor of God (verse 13). No need for amazing feats of strength! Simply be still and stand. The I AM is with you.

> *Every day begins with an act of courage and hope:*
> *getting out of bed.*
> MASON COOLEY

To Do

Put on your spiritual armor— even if your "shoes of peace" have orthopedic insoles. And make a list of every battle God has victoriously brought you through. Keep it handy for encouragement in the next battle.

"As long as I'm not
six feet under."

16

TO BE OR NOT TO BE, THAT IS THE QUESTION

The creation looks forward to the day when it will join
God's children in glorious freedom from death and decay.
For we know that all creation has been groaning as
in the pains of childbirth right up to the present time.

ROMANS 8:21-22

At my very first service as a newly graduated youth pastor, the senior pastor mentioned during prayer time a "senior saint" who was in critical condition at a nursing home and wanted to go Home—with a capital H.

He then turned in my direction and asked me to pray for the woman. And so I rather awkwardly prayed that God would ease her suffering through healing, or if it was his will, to take her Home. (I figured I'd give God some options.)

About five minutes later, the church phone rang and the secretary slipped out to answer it. She came back with a dazed and bewildered look and interrupted the sermon. "Uh . . . Pastor. It was the nursing home. Sister Smith . . . uh . . . passed away about five minutes ago."

Suddenly, this wet-behind-the-ears pastor had clergy

credibility! (Not that I wanted to be known as "Reverend Death.")

A few years later, my grandmother was in the hospital. After a wonderful visit reminiscing about the good old days, I gave her a kiss on the forehead and told her I loved her and would be praying for her. As I walked to the door, she called out, "Pray that I die tonight." I kept walking as if I hadn't heard!

Maybe that is your prayer as well. My great-grandmother, grandmother, and mother all asked God to take them Home rather than to continue in their physical suffering. But they—and you—are not alone. Paul writes:

> I fully expect and hope that I will never be ashamed, but that I will continue to be bold for Christ, as I have been in the past. And I trust that my life will bring honor to Christ, whether I live or die. For to me, living means living for Christ, and dying is even better. But if I live, I can do more fruitful work for Christ. So I really don't know which is better. I'm torn between two desires: I long to go and be with Christ, which would be far better for me. But for your sakes, it is better that I continue to live.
>
> Knowing this, I am convinced that I will remain alive so I can continue to help all of you grow and experience the joy of your faith.

PHILIPPIANS 1:20-25

I understood that tension when I was writhing on the emergency room gurney with my kidney stone. It felt as if a logging truck with tire chains had parked on my lower back. Between bouts of vomiting from the pain, I prayed, "Jesus, take me! Take me *now*!"

Be assured, I do understand pain. I understand complete depletion of strength after forty-two daily radiation treatments. I understand feeling hopeless with depression. I get it. But I also firmly believe that if I wake up in the morning or from my afternoon nap, God has something meaningful and significant for me to do for him. And that gives me strength to get out of bed.

Dearly loved friends, we would free ourselves from great fears in this life if we would simply fear death! We should live now so at the hour of death we may rejoice rather than cower. We must learn to die to the world now, so we can begin to live with Christ now.

THOMAS À KEMPIS

To Do

Jot down reasons why, as the apostle Paul writes, "it is better that I continue to live."

PART IV

CURIOSITY

Continued to explore this amazing, miraculous world that God has created, knowing that our minds can stay young by learning new things.

The people of Berea were more open-minded than those in Thessalonica, and they listened eagerly to Paul's message. They searched the Scriptures day after day to see if Paul and Silas were teaching the truth.

ACTS 17:11

"Then one day,
I became curious."

17

CURIOSITY KILLS ONLY CATS

"This is amazing," Moses said to himself.
"Why isn't that bush burning up? I must go see it."

EXODUS 3:3

The earliest printed form of "Curiosity killed the cat" is attributed to British playwright Ben Jonson's 1598 play, *Every Man in His Humour*: "Care killed the cat."

Many years later, the March 4, 1916, edition of the *Washington Post* documented an actual case headlined: CURIOSITY KILLED THE CAT. (It must have been a slow news day.) Miss Mable Godfrey reported that "Blackie," an indoor feline, squeezed through the fireplace screen and climbed up the chimney flue, where he refused to budge. Despite efforts by the police, fire, health, and building departments, the cat refused to come down. Sadly, three days later Blackie fell to his death.

While curiosity does indeed kill cats, it has been the secret to all the great social movements, all the great inventions and medical discoveries, and the ability to stay mentally young.

For instance, what would have happened if Moses, upon seeing the burning bush, had run away screaming in terror? What if he had simply walked by, shaking his head. "Hmmph. That's really weird." What if, when he heard the voice from the bush, he muttered, "I've been out here in the desert way too long!" and headed for home.

We would not have the Exodus from Egypt, the Ten Commandments, or the first five books of the Bible. Thankfully, Moses was curious! "This is amazing! Why isn't that bush burning up? I must go see it."

So here are some inspirational quotations and fun facts on curiosity to stimulate your brain cells:

"Anyone who stops learning is old, whether at twenty or eighty. Anyone who keeps learning stays young. The greatest thing in life is to keep your mind young" (Henry Ford).[24]

Aldous Huxley wrote to his brother: "It is hard to feel old. . . . We both, I think, belong to that fortunate minority of human beings, who retain the mental openness and elasticity of youth, while being able to enjoy the fruits of an already long experience."[25]

Christopher Bergland wrote in *Psychology Today*:

Recent psychological studies have confirmed that staying curious is not only the key to maintaining a sense of wonder and appreciation for life—it is the key to your success. Remaining conscientious is equally important. In fact, the combined personality traits of being *curious and conscientious* were found to be more important than intelligence in predicting success. . . .

Once you become jaded, you no longer attack problems and challenges with enthusiasm and inquisitiveness. It's easy to get sucked into the ho-hum mindset of mediocrity.[26]

Edith Wharton declared, "In spite of illness, in spite even of the archenemy sorrow, one can remain alive long past the usual date of disintegration if one is unafraid of change, insatiable in intellectual curiosity, interested in big things, and happy in small ways."[27]

So to stay young, stay curious . . . and avoid chimney flues.

I have no special talents. I am only passionately curious.
ALBERT EINSTEIN

To Do

Be curious.

"Let me suggest, Pastor,
if you haven't hit oil in
the first twenty minutes,
stop boring."

18

BORED TO DEATH

How much better to get wisdom than gold,
and good judgment than silver!

PROVERBS 16:16

Growing up in the country, I never ever whined, "I'm bored." If I did, my parents would thrust a hoe, rake, or snow shovel into my idle hands!

In this amazing world, we should never be bored to death. In fact, *lifelong learning* is the key to an interesting life. It is the formal or informal accumulation of knowledge post-graduation and throughout one's lifetime. It can be done via a community college class, watching a documentary, or simply reading a book. Congratulations, you're being a life-long learner right this very second!

The Good News

University of California, Irvine neurobiologist Lulu Chen discovered "a critical relationship between learning and brain growth."[28] Additional research has proven that continual learning keeps brain cells working at optimum levels and limits cognitive and memory decline.[29] But wait, there's more! It also reduces depression in all ages.[30]

And for those diagnosed with early-onset Alzheimer's disease, there's even more good news! Dr. Penny Dacks, a neuroscientist and director of Aging and Alzheimer's Disease Prevention at the Alzheimer's Drug Discovery Foundation, writes: "A new study in *JAMA Neurology* . . . specifically looked at people who carry the . . . genetic risk factor for Alzheimer's disease. . . . Carriers with a high level of lifetime intellectual enrichment were shown to have their cognitive impairment delayed by almost nine years on average."[31]

Lifelong learning also includes improvement in personal and professional skills. Valamis, which dubs itself "A Learning Experience Platform," promises:

> While we're busy learning a new skill or acquiring new knowledge, we're also building other valuable skills that can help us in our personal and professional lives.
>
> This is because we utilize other skills in order to learn something new. For example, learning to sew requires problem-solving. Learning to draw involves developing creativity.
>
> Skill development can include interpersonal skills, creativity, problem-solving, critical thinking, leadership, reflection, adaptability and much more.[32]

Saamah Abdallah, a senior researcher at the New Economic Foundation's Centre for Wellbeing, adds these benefits to continual learning: "It can boost your self-esteem and show you that you can do things. But it also builds that sense of autonomy, and a lot of learning happens in groups, in classes and courses which, if done well, means people can build relationships too."[33]

More Good News

There are thousands of free resources available to keep your brain in the best shape possible: adult education programs, affordable classes to audit at colleges, and free online courses, to name a few. And don't forget—one of my favorite places on earth—libraries. Don't let visual challenges stop you. There are thousands of large-print and audio resources available.

So if you want to grow brain cells, improve your memory, lessen depression, expand your skills, and delay the onset of Alzheimer's for up to nine years, become a lifelong learner.

It's what you learn after you know it all that counts.
HARRY S. TRUMAN

To Do
Watch. Listen. Read. Repeat.

PART V

FAITH, HOPE & LOVE

Sought through Bible study, prayer, and fellowship with others to improve our conscious contact with God.

Three things will last forever—faith, hope, and love—and the greatest of these is love.

1 CORINTHIANS 13:13

"I'm about to give
her a facelift."

19

EVERYONE NEEDS
A FAITH-LIFT

Faith shows the reality of what we hope for;
it is the evidence of things we cannot see.
Through their faith, the people in days
of old earned a good reputation.

HEBREWS 11:1-2

The American Society of Plastic Surgeons reports that nearly two million major cosmetic surgical procedures are performed each year in the United States.[34] I have a better idea. A faith-lift! Here's a side-by-side comparison:

Benefits

Facelifts: According to the American Board of Cosmetic Surgery (ABCS), "A facelift surgery can help a patient look not just younger, but simply 'better.'"[35]

Faith-lifts: According to the apostle Paul, faith doesn't repair us but remakes us! "This means that anyone who belongs to Christ has become a new person. The old life is gone; a new life has begun!" (2 Corinthians 5:17).

Complications

Facelifts will produce bruising and swelling, which normally peak about two days after surgery and diminish in usually ten to fourteen days. Serious side effects can include—in alphabetical order—bleeding, bruising, complications with anesthesia, damage to the facial nerves controlling muscles (which is usually temporary), hematoma, infection, loss of hair around the incision site, numbness, scarring, skin necrosis (death of tissue), unevenness between two sides of the face, and widening or thickening of scar.[36]

Faith-lifts will produce no harmful side effects. In fact, here's the best way to get rid of those dark spots! "Those who look to [God] for help will be radiant with joy; no shadow of shame will darken their faces" (Psalm 34:5).

Longevity

Facelifts have a limited life span. Five and a half years after surgery, 21 percent of facelifts will relapse, but 76 percent of people still look younger.[37] A full facelift can last up to fifteen years, with less invasive techniques lasting anywhere from two to six years.[38]

Faith-lifts have an eternal life span: "I tell you the truth, those who listen to my message and believe in God who sent me have eternal life. They will never be condemned for their sins, but they have already passed from death into life" (John 5:24).

Costs

Facelifts: According to the ABCS, actual surgical costs range from $7,700 to $11,780.[39] But like a batteries-not-included warning, this does not include an anesthesia fee, hospital costs, and other medical expenses. Total costs can easily exceed $15,000 and—you guessed it—are not covered by insurance.[40]

Faith-lifts cost us nothing! According to the Bible, "God saved you by his grace when you believed. And you can't take credit for this; it is a gift from God. Salvation is not a reward for the good things we have done, so none of us can boast about it" (Ephesians 2:8-9).

> *The beauty of a woman is not in a facial mole,*
> *but true beauty in a woman is reflected in her soul.*
> *It is the caring that she lovingly gives,*
> *the passion that she knows.*
>
> AUDREY HEPBURN

To Do

Start a daily beauty routine—or manly workout—for your soul.

"I installed the peephole backwards.
Now all my troubles seem so far away."

2 0

A HOPE AND A FUTURE

"I know the plans I have for you," says the LORD.
"They are plans for good and not for disaster,
to give you a future and a hope."

JEREMIAH 29:11

Many believers claim today's promise in Jeremiah as their favorite verse. But they may not know "the rest of the story."

King Josiah had been killed in a battle against the invading Egyptian army on its way to Babylon. While Josiah was the poster child for a godly king, history records his son Johoiachin was a godless tyrant who had incestuous relationships with his mother, daughter-in-law, and stepmother, while murdering his subjects, taking their property, and raping their wives.

King Nebuchadnezzar of Babylon crushed the Egyptians and then turned on Judah. He besieged Jerusalem in 609 BC and demanded protection money from King Jehoiachin. During this first invasion, during which Daniel and his friends were forcibly taken to Babylon, Jeremiah wrote a letter to Johoiachin confronting his immoral actions: "The LORD has punished Jerusalem for her many sins" (Lamentations 1:5).

In 598 BC, Babylon invaded again, killing the king and taking more POWs.

Thus begins Jeremiah 29: "Jeremiah wrote a letter from Jerusalem to the elders, priests, prophets, and all the people who had been exiled to Babylon by King Nebuchadnezzar."

But things got even worse in Judah!

> Likewise, all the leaders of the priests and the people became more and more unfaithful. They followed all the pagan practices of the surrounding nations, desecrating the Temple of the LORD that had been consecrated in Jerusalem.
>
> The LORD . . . repeatedly sent his prophets to warn them, for he had compassion on his people and his Temple. But the people mocked these messengers of God and despised their words.
>
> 2 CHRONICLES 36:14-16

During this time, Nebuchadnezzar installed twenty-one-year-old Zedekiah as a puppet king, but the new king attempted once again to ally with the Egyptians. (Had the Israelites learned nothing in their relationship with Egypt?) This prompted a brutal siege by the Babylonians, which some scholars believe lasted up to two and a half years with Jerusalem completely surrounded and cut off from croplands. People starving to death inside the walled city actually turned to cannibalism (Lamentations 4:3-10).

This time, the walls of Jerusalem were completely destroyed, and Solomon's Temple totally leveled. King Zedekiah's sons were executed before him, before his own eyes were gouged out, and he was hauled off to prison.

"And your point is, Jim?" The promise of Jeremiah 29:11 is for the up-to-twenty-thousand Hebrews who were taken out of Judah before God's wrath was poured out on the immoral kings, priests, and citizens who had fallen back into idolatry. In "captivity," they were spared the severest of God's judgment and could return seventy years later with a "hope and a future."

You do not need to know precisely what
is happening, or exactly where it is all going.
What you need is to recognize the possibilities and
challenges offered by the present moment, and
to embrace them with courage, faith, and hope.

THOMAS MERTON

To Do

Write down incidents that seemed disastrous at the time and how God was actually protecting you from something far worse. Believe he will do it again!

"Laughter *is* the best medicine . . .
but I'm not in your HMO."

21

LAUGHTER IS THE BEST OVER-THE-COUNTER MEDICINE

A cheerful heart is good medicine.

PROVERBS 17:22

As far back as the reign of Solomon from around 970 to 930 BC, humor has been known for its healing properties. Voltaire, a French writer and philosopher from the 1700s, noted: "The art of medicine consists in amusing the patient, while nature cures the disease."[41] More recently, Dr. Paul E. McGhee, in his book *Health, Healing and the Amuse System*, documents the health benefits of humor:

Humor strengthens the immune system. Laughter increases immunoglobulin A, a part of your immune system that protects you against upper respiratory problems, like colds and the flu. Humor also increases T-cells, which seek out and destroy tumor cells, viruses, and foreign organisms.

Humor reduces food cravings. I'll have to do more study on that as soon as I finish my daily dosage of dark-chocolate-covered coffee beans.[42]

Humor reduces pain and increases one's threshold for pain. Norman Cousins's book *Anatomy of an Illness as Perceived by the Patient* documents how a spinal disease left him in almost constant pain. He discovered that moving out of a dreary hospital and into a cheery hotel room, where he watched *Candid Camera* and comedy films, eased his pain. He specifically denied that humor "cured" anything and repeatedly reminded his readers that he took all the medications prescribed by his doctors.

But he did claim in his last book, *Head First: The Biology of Hope*, that ten minutes of belly laughter gave him two hours of pain-free sleep.[43]

Over a dozen studies have now documented that humor does have the power to reduce pain in many patients. One study published in the *New England Journal of Medicine* surveyed thirty-five patients in a rehabilitation hospital suffering from such conditions as traumatic brain injury, spinal cord injury, arthritis, limb amputations, and a range of other neurological or musculoskeletal disorders. Nearly three-fourths (74 percent) agreed with the statement, "Sometimes, laughter works as well as a pain pill."[44]

Humor reduces the level of stress hormones. Cortisol, epinephrine (adrenaline), dopamine, and growth hormone are all produced during the "flight or fight" response when you encounter a grizzly bear or find yourself in other frightful situations. Laughter reduces these chemicals and promotes calmness.

Humor is a cardiovascular workout. Some have called laughter "internal jogging," which may reduce blood pressure. There's even an emerging therapeutic field known as "humor therapy."[45]

Let me prescribe the following: Hang around people with a great sense of humor. I divide people into two categories: life-lifters and soul-crushers. As the names imply, life-lifters are positive people with a great sense of humor while soul-crushers do just that. They squeeze all the energy out of your spirit with their negativity and lack of humor.

Then claim the promise given to Job, who was definitely having a bad day: "He will once again fill your mouth with laughter and your lips with shouts of joy" (Job 8:21).

*The secret of life lies
in laughter and humility.*
G.K. CHESTERTON

To Do
Laugh!

"I jumped in this fountain of youth
and had to have a hip replacement."

LOVE IS THE FOUNTAIN OF YOUTH

Dear friends, let us continue to love one another,
for love comes from God. Anyone who loves is
a child of God and knows God.

1 JOHN 4:7

Ben Franklin wrote, "Those who love deeply never grow old; they may die of old age, but they die young."

The Bible goes even further to tell us that because of God's love, we can live forever (John 3:16).

Here are some other important things the Bible says about love:

Love Comes from God

Many people think that God is only interested in rules. But God is all about love. Jesus, God the Son, reminds us of the most important "rule":

Jesus replied, "'You must love the LORD your God with all your heart, all your soul, and all your mind.' This is the first and greatest commandment. A second is equally important: 'Love your neighbor as yourself.'"

MATTHEW 22:37-39

"Okay," we say. "That sounds good." But we seem powerless to love like that.

> If someone says, "I love God," but hates a fellow believer, that person is a liar; for if we don't love people we can see, how can we love God, whom we cannot see? And he has given us this command: Those who love God must also love their fellow believers.
>
> I JOHN 4:20-21

Love Keeps Us Forever Young

> God is love, and all who live in love live in God, and God lives in them.
>
> I JOHN 4:16

Think about that for a moment. God is love. God is eternal. And because God is not limited by time, he hasn't aged one single day! He is forever young! And if you really want to stretch your mind—right out of your skull—consider that God who has no beginning or end is actually younger than you! And because we live in God and he in us, we too can be forever young. BOOM! Mind blown.

Sin is what ages our spirit. However, God's only Son, Jesus

Christ, died and rose again to atone for our unloving behavior (1 John 2:1-2). *Atone* means to make "at-one" with. When we confess our lack of love (sin) and believe that Christ has died and risen for our sin, we are forgiven and are "at one" with God and his love (1 John 1:9). God abides in those who confess that Jesus is the Son of God, and they abide in God (1 John 4:15).

Remember 2 Corinthians 4:16? "Though our bodies are dying, our spirits are being *renewed* every day" (emphasis mine). The Greek verb *anakainoō* means "to renew," and occurs only in this verse and Colossians 3:10: "Put on your new nature, and be renewed as you learn to know your Creator and become like him." Both times it refers to the *continual, never-ending, ever-transforming* power of God in the believer's spirit.

In him, we can sing at the top of our lungs, "Forever young!"

Love like there's no tomorrow.

JNW

To Do

If you have never invited God into your life through the work of Jesus, please do that today.

"I love my neighbor as myself.
I'm single and I live in the mountains."

23

LOVING YOURSELF AS YOUR NEIGHBOR

*Jesus replied, "'You must love the LORD your God
with all your heart, all your soul, and all your mind.'
This is the first and greatest commandment. A second is
equally important: 'Love your neighbor as yourself.'"*

MATTHEW 22:37-39

The Bible provides a lengthy list of directions for obeying the
second great command, to love our neighbors. Please take
out a number 2 pencil and check the following boxes that
apply to you. (You will be graded on this!)

☐ "Be patient with each other, making allowance for each
other's faults because of your love." (Ephesians 4:2)

☐ "Encourage each other and build each other up."
(1 Thessalonians 5:11)

☐ "Be kind to each other, tenderhearted, forgiving one
another, just as God through Christ has forgiven
you." (Ephesians 4:32)

☐ "Clothe yourselves with tenderhearted mercy,
kindness, humility, gentleness, and patience. Make

allowance for each other's faults, and forgive anyone who offends you. Remember, the Lord forgave you, so you must forgive others. Above all, clothe yourselves with love, which binds us all together in perfect harmony." (Colossians 3:12-14)

☐ "Don't use foul or abusive language. Let everything you say be good and helpful, so that your words will be an encouragement to those who hear them." (Ephesians 4:29)

☐ "Stop telling lies. Let us tell our neighbors the truth." (Ephesians 4:25)

☐ "Speak the truth in love." (Ephesians 4:15)

☐ "We should help others do what is right and build them up in the Lord." (Romans 15:2)

How did you do? Okay, that's a trick question, because this devotional is not about how you treat your neighbor. Nope! I want to ask you this important question: Do you treat yourself as well as you treat your neighbor?

Are you patient with yourself? Can you forgive yourself? Are you merciful, kind, and gentle with yourself? Do you encourage yourself, or do you use "foul or abusive language" in your self-talk? Are you building yourself up in the Lord? And most of all, do you love yourself as God loves you?

If you're going to love your neighbor as yourself, you're going to have to first love yourself. Now don't go all self-righteous, super spiritual, or falsely humble and quote Isaac Watts's hymn about being "such a worm as I." We are creations of the holy and perfect God. And when he created humans, he proclaimed them "very good." Not "good" like the other five days' work, but *very* good.

I insult God when I say things to myself that I would never think to say to my neighbor: "I'm such an idiot!" "How can I be so stupid?!" "You are . . ." Well, you get the idea. I need to give myself some love, and I can only do that reminding myself that Christ first loved me and provided forgiveness and calls me his friend. Yeah, me—a friend of the Son of God!

So from now on, let's love ourselves as we love our neighbor.

Don't belittle yourself. Be BIG yourself.
CORITA KENT

To Do

Make a list of all the things you like about yourself. And don't be afraid to be brutally honest. You really are a very likable person!

PART VI

FORGIVENESS

Made a list of all persons we
had harmed and those we had
held grudges against and became
willing to make amends with
anyone we called "an old goat."

*If you forgive those who sin against you,
your heavenly Father will forgive you.*

MATTHEW 6:14

"Pastor, if I love my enemies,
do I have to kiss 'em?"

24

LOVE YOUR ENEMIES—
IT WILL FREAK THEM OUT

*Love your enemies! Do good to them. Lend to them without
expecting to be repaid. Then your reward from heaven will be
very great, and you will truly be acting as children of the Most High.*

LUKE 6:35

I had the opportunity to teach writing in India for three weeks
with Cec Murphey. To my surprise, one weeklong seminar
was attended not only by Christians, but also Hindus and
Muslims.

Our hosts treated us as "honored guests" with huge flo-
ral leis that made us look like the winning horses at the
Kentucky Derby, and a British-style afternoon tea complete
with crumpets and generous gifts. But during this week, we
also were treated to a heckler.

"What are you American Christians doing here teaching
us Hindus?" a man shouted from the back row.

Cec graciously replied, "This class will be helpful for all of
you whether you are Christian, Muslim, Hindu, or atheist.
Good writing is good writing no matter what your faith."

At the break, Cec whispered to me, "We're going to love that man. There is no defense against love." And so at lunchtime, Cec and I made our way to the man's table and asked if we could join him. Our question seemed to shock him, but he agreed. After a few awkward minutes, he lowered his defenses a bit and began asking questions about writing. As the week progressed, he began sitting closer and closer to the front. And no more heckling!

As we were packing up our books and notes at the end of the last class, our heckler approached us with a friend holding a camera. "Here," he said to his friend, "take a picture of me and my American friends." He wrapped his big arms around us and smiled for the camera. "Thank you for coming, friends."

Cec was right—there is no defense against love.

You may not have anyone in your life you consider an enemy, but there are probably enough people who have hurt or insulted you that you may hold resentment toward or grudges against. Jesus makes it very clear that we are to love and forgive everyone . . . even our enemies.

Anne Lamott powerfully illustrates just how deadly unforgiveness is in our lives: "Not forgiving is like drinking rat poison and then waiting for the rat to die."[46]

The rat feels absolutely no effect of your anger and resentment. He or she may not even remember the offense that you keep replaying in your mind. But you feel the poison affecting not only your relationship but your interactions with others.

Unforgiveness will damage not only your spiritual life, but your physical life as well. Dr. Loren Toussaint, a professor of psychology at Luther College in Iowa, warns that "a brew of bitterness, hostility, and revenge" has major consequences. A reporter on Toussaint's work summarizes that it triggers "anxiety, depression, digestive issues, trouble sleeping, weight gain, a weakened immune response, and even heart problems."[47]

There is power and freedom in forgiving and being forgiven!

Returning hate for hate multiplies hate, adding deeper darkness to a night already devoid of stars. Darkness cannot drive out darkness; only light can do that. Hate cannot drive out hate; only love can do that.

MARTIN LUTHER KING JR.

To Do

Forgive.

"I lost my job at the gym.
I just wasn't working out."

25

I'M A MESS. YOU'RE A MESS. THAT'S WHY WE HAVE A MESSIAH!

I'm a muddy mess.

JOB 30:19, MSG

At a conference, I shared that this "award-winning author" and "international speaker" is one great big slobbering *mess*.

I have clinical depression, OCD, ADD, and . . . what was I saying? Oh yes, I'm on the autistic spectrum: I don't like having my rigid routine disrupted (I need twenty-four-hour notice to be spontaneous), and I hate traveling and being in new situations. Plus, although I love people, being around them drains my emotional batteries. (I'm an off-the-chart introvert on the Myers-Briggs assessment.) And so this outgoing, outspoken, outrageous author/speaker is, in reality, an introverted, inadequate, and insecure actor giving an Oscar-worthy performance.

After my confession, I asked the people in the audience to turn to the person on their right and say, "I'm a mess." Then I asked them to turn to the person on their left and say, "You're a mess." When I finished the keynote address, a woman came up to me in tears and gave me a hug. Well, it was more like a bear hug. Actually, a *grizzly* bear hug! She sobbed uncontrollably. "I'm so glad someone besides me is a mess."

It is liberating to realize, "I'm a mess. You're a mess." In fact, that should come as no surprise.

> Everyone has sinned; we all fall short of God's glorious standard.
>
> ROMANS 3:23

> When we display our righteous deeds, they are nothing but filthy rags.
>
> ISAIAH 64:6

> The temptations in your life are no different from what others experience.
>
> I CORINTHIANS 10:13

> [Jesus] told them, "Healthy people don't need a doctor—sick people do. I have come to call not those who think they are righteous, but those who know they are sinners."
>
> MARK 2:17

> We are unworthy servants.
>
> LUKE 17:10

But here's the wonderful *mess*-age for all of us messes: *We have a Mess-iah!*

Just look at the messes that God has chosen to use: Moses wasn't a speaker. Gideon was the least of his tribe. Daniel was a POW. Jeremiah was depressed and suicidal. Peter had a severe case of "hoof-in-mouth" disease. James and John were hot-heads living up to their nicknames "Sons of Thunder." The woman at the well was the original "Desperate Housewife." Paul had a "thorn in the flesh." Mark was a quitter. Timothy was timid and sickly.

So be encouraged. The Messiah can empower and use messes like you and me for his purposes. Paul writes:

When I first came to you, dear brothers and sisters,
I didn't use lofty words and impressive wisdom to
tell you God's secret plan. For I decided that while I
was with you I would forget everything except Jesus
Christ, the one who was crucified. I came to you in
weakness—timid and trembling. And my message
and my preaching were very plain. Rather than
using clever and persuasive speeches, I relied only
on the power of the Holy Spirit. I did this so you
would trust not in human wisdom but in the power
of God.

1 CORINTHIANS 2:1-5

Ready? Repeat after me, please: "I'm a mess. You're a mess." And then proclaim, "That's why we have a Messiah."

People are messy; therefore, relationships will be messy.
Don't be surprised by messiness.
TIMOTHY KELLER

To Do

Admit to yourself and a trusted friend, "I'm a mess."

PART VII

GRATITUDE

We're entirely ready to have
God remove all our wrong
attitudes toward aging and
replace them with thanksgiving
for his loving care over us.

Let the peace that comes from Christ rule in your hearts.
. . . And always be thankful.

COLOSSIANS 3:15

"Pastor, would you tell my husband that crab apples, prunes, and lemons are not fruit of the Spirit?"

26

CRAB APPLES ARE NOT A FRUIT OF THE SPIRIT

The Holy Spirit produces this kind of fruit in our lives: love, joy, peace, patience, kindness, goodness, faithfulness, gentleness, and self-control. There is no law against these things!

GALATIANS 5:22-23

Elsie Drummonds was one of the most influential people in my teenaged life. My pastor's wife was gracious, elegant, and deeply in love with Jesus and people of all ages. Later, when her husband was asked to oversee a district in our denomination and eventually served at the church headquarters, Elsie continued to encourage and mentor hundreds if not thousands of individuals. Then, when she was diagnosed with cancer and went to an assisted living facility, she made it her new mission field. We kept in touch throughout the years, and I depended on her encouragement and powerful prayers through my forty-five years of writing and speaking.

Just before she died of cancer at age eighty-eight, her son-in-love asked her how he could pray for her. She immediately answered, "Pray that I don't get grumpy." He testified at her funeral that despite her painful death, her prayer was answered.

That's my prayer as well! Unfortunately, many seniors don't ripen—they rot. They seem to think that crab apples, prunes, and lemons are fruit of the Spirit. I mentioned in the introduction that God wants to renew us spiritually and empower us so we may "still bear fruit in old age [and] stay fresh and green" (Psalm 92:14, NIV).

That fruit is only possible by the infilling of the Holy Spirit as Paul explains in Galatians 5. He provides a handy list for inspecting fruit:

- ☐ love
- ☐ joy
- ☐ peace
- ☐ patience
- ☐ kindness
- ☐ goodness
- ☐ faithfulness
- ☐ gentleness
- ☐ self-control

If this list seems overwhelming, please try something. If you have a fruit tree nearby, go out and put your ear up against the trunk. Okay. Now, listen carefully. Do you hear grunting and groaning as the tree strains to squeeze out its fruit? If you do, seek immediate psychiatric attention!

As long as a tree is receiving adequate water, nutrients, and sunlight, it will *naturally* produce fruit. That's all it can do! So here's the secret straight from Jesus:

> Remain in me, and I will remain in you. For a branch cannot produce fruit if it is severed from the vine, and you cannot be fruitful unless you remain in me.
>
> Yes, I am the vine; you are the branches. Those who remain in me, and I in them, will produce much fruit.

JOHN 15:4-5

When we keep connected to Jesus through Bible study, prayer, worship, service, and fellowship with other believers, the fruit of the Spirit will naturally grow.

May you be fruitful no matter where you find yourself planted, because you are attached to the Vine—the very Son of God.

What will it be? New wine or old whine?

JNW

To Do

Select a Spirit-given fruit to cultivate this week.

At the senior fellowship time,
discussion revolves around where
to find the best prescription prices.

27

I'M EIGHT
PILL BOTTLES OLD

*Don't drink only water. You ought to drink a little wine
for the sake of your stomach because you are sick so often.*

1 TIMOTHY 5:23

You can tell the age of a tree by counting the rings on the trunk. With a horse, you can count its teeth. Scientists can even use carbon dating to determine the age of rocks and Uncle Harold. Here's a theory, courtesy of *moi*: You can tell people's age by counting the number of pill bottles in their medicine cabinet.

One pill: One to thirteen years

From ages one to sixteen, my one pill a day was Flintstones chewable vitamins. Actually, I started out on something akin to *I Love Lucy*'s "Vitameatavegamin." Each morning, my mom would tackle me, pin me to the floor, and force a tablespoon of Vitagagachokearetch down my throat.

Two pills: Fourteen to nineteen years

At fourteen, my hormones waged war against my body, and suddenly my face erupted into full-scale, thermonuclear acne.

Add to that a set of old-school metal braces and I looked like a pepperoni pizza with a zipper. Fortunately, there were tetracycline pills, which brought a bit of peace to my war-ravaged face.

Three pills: Twenty to twenty-nine years

In my twenties, I discovered I had inherited my mother's and grandmother's arthritis in my neck and fingers. My grandmother's fingers were so twisted she could pull the cork from a wine bottle with her pinkie. So I added Extra Strength Tylenol to the medicine cabinet.

Four pills: Thirty to thirty-nine years

When I hit thirty, my cholesterol hit 307. That's roughly the number for a four-hundred-pound couch potato whose diet consists only of pork rinds and deep-fried Twinkies. Since I weighed 150, rode a bike, and tried to eat right, I was prescribed meds, and my cholesterol promptly dropped below 200. I also added two antidepressants to the medicine cabinet (more about that in chapter 31).

Seven pills: Forty to forty-nine years

At forty, I added glucosamine chondroitin to keep my fingers from turning into corkscrews, a low-dose aspirin to prevent heart attacks, and Zyrtec for living in northern Indiana—which I suspect is the pollen capital of North America.

Eight pills: Fifty years and up

It got even worse at fifty. I actually bought one of those divided pillboxes with the day of the week on each compartment. I might as well have tattooed GEEZER across my forehead! I'm now in possession of more drugs than a meth dealer.

So here's my point—and I really do have one.

We live in an amazing age when we can survive and thrive with illness and chronic conditions that would have incapacitated or killed off our ancestors. I am grateful for my anti-allergy, anti-blood clot, anti-cholesterol, anti-inflammation, and anti-depression drugs. Without them, my arteries would be clogged like a Drano ad and I'd be sitting in the dark writing awful poetry about pain, death, and postnasal drip. Plus, someone else's name would be on this book's cover.

"Better Living Through Chemistry"
DOW CHEMICAL COMPANY

To Do

As you take your meds today,
thank God for each pill
and the specific relief it offers.

"I was counting my blessings and,
so far, I'm up to infinity."

28

FIFTY REASONS TO GIVE THANKS

*Give thanks for everything to God the Father
in the name of our Lord Jesus Christ.*

EPHESIANS 5:20

One morning, I vowed not to ask for anything in prayer, but to simply praise God. Fifty things came to mind—and were offered to him—just between the bed and bathroom:

1. God's protection and providence
2. His love and grace
3. Sleeping straight through the night
4. No horrible nightmares resulting from real-life trauma
5. Not working the night shift like in college
6. My CPAP (continuous positive airway pressure) machine that keeps me from dying of asphyxia
7. Hearing my phone alarm
8. Smartphone—although mine seems to do dumb things!

9. Seeing my smartphone
10. Waking up in a warm waterbed with flannel sheets (it's January)
11. Heat (and central air during the summer)
12. The house is paid off.
13. Waking up refreshed
14. Pain level below 2 despite arthritis
15. Clean air
16. Electricity
17. Cardinals singing
18. Being able to click "snooze" because of working at home
19. Two working hands and arms
20. Pulling up the covers and rolling over
21. Getting out of bed unassisted
22. Not waking up in North Korea
23. Not waking up in a war-torn country
24. Not waking up in prison
25. Not waking up in a hospital
26. Not waking up in a nursing home
27. Walking unassisted: no crutches, walkers, braces, or casts
28. Lots of clothes in the closet—and on the floor
29. Walking on carpeting rather than dirt
30. Being able to feel the carpet under my toes
31. A loving family

32. A loving, faithful Christian wife
33. Children who love Jesus
34. Kids who are gainfully employed in serving others and God
35. No one in my family is currently incarcerated!
36. Eight grandkiddos
37. The picture on the wall of my three-year-old daughter with a mischievous grin. It always makes me smile.
38. Being able to work from home since 1982
39. Hundreds of advantages of being self-employed, such as being there for wife, kids, and grandkids in good and bad times
40. Computers: A love/hate relationship, but I wouldn't be a writer if I had to do all that retyping!
41. Solid oak desk that my dad and I made while I was in high school
42. Social media
43. Meaningful service for God
44. Meaningful work—at least today (in Freelance Land, it's either feast or famine)
45. Remembering where the bathroom is. No Alzheimer's—yet.
46. Indoor plumbing
47. My own "plumbing" that is in fine working order after successful radiation for prostate cancer!

48. Being able to read (I always have books and magazines in the "reading room")
49. Freedom of the press
50. Toilet paper (remember the COVID-19 crisis of 2020?)

There is no way I am going to age gracefully,
but I do hope to age gratefully.

JNW

To Do

Make your own list of all the reasons you have to give God thanks.
(Don't stop at fifty!)

AGERS ANONYMOUS

PART VIII

JOY

Humbly asked God to swap our
complaints with things that
help us experience his joy.

I will be glad and rejoice in your unfailing love,
for you have seen my troubles,
and you care about the anguish of my soul.

PSALM 31:7

"I wish he was full of joy.
Most days, he's full of 'oy.'"

29

WHEN YOUR ONLY JOY
IS UNDER THE SINK

Satisfy us each morning with your unfailing love,
so we may sing for joy to the end of our lives.

PSALM 90:14

Do you ever have days when your only "Joy" is the dish-washing liquid?

We've all been there, even though we can recite Philippians 4:4 from memory: "Rejoice in the Lord alway: and again I say, Rejoice" (KJV).

Then we feel even less joyful, knowing that we're falling short of Paul's admonition. And to be totally discouraged, read the words of James, the brother of Jesus: "Dear brothers and sisters, when troubles of any kind come your way, consider it an opportunity for great joy" (James 1:2).

But wait, there's more! Paul gives us details about what he's gone through: "Five different times the Jewish leaders gave me thirty-nine lashes. Three times I was beaten with rods. Once I was stoned. Three times I was shipwrecked. Once I spent a whole night and a day adrift at sea" (2 Corinthians 11:24-25).

Here I am complaining about my aching back when Paul has had his lashed with a whip 195 times, beaten with rods three times, and pounded with stones. While I whine about the arthritis in my neck, James had his severed with a sword!

Okay, okay, I get it, Jim! I should feel joyful. Well, that is the problem:

Joy is not a feeling

We may not feel *happy*, but God has promised *joy*. Think of happiness as a bobber floating on the surface of the ocean. It rises and falls, depending on the size of the waves. The higher the highs, the lower the lows. That often describes our emotions.

However, if you were able to see a cross section of the ocean, you would see a jellyfish floating just a few feet below the raging waves. The water at that level is perfectly still. That is joy.

Happiness is an emotion. Joy is an attitude. That's why Jesus could make this promise to his disciples—just before his brutal death: "I have told you these things so that you will be filled with my joy. Yes, your joy will overflow!" (John 15:11).

Emotions are real, but not reality

That's what I want you to remember from this chapter. Admit that you are grieving, feeling depressed, discouraged, etc.

Those emotions are real. But they are not the reality found in the joy of Christ. Your emotions are bobbing up and down on the overwhelming waves in your earthly situation. But deep in your soul, you have the stability of knowing that God is in control, he loves you unconditionally, and we're assured in Psalm 30:5 that he will turn sorrowful mourning into a joyful morning!

My life has been filled with
more sorrow than I ever feared . . .
and more joy than I ever dreamed.

JNW

To Do

Allow yourself to honestly express your raging emotions. Then allow Jesus to supernaturally calm the storm with his love, comfort, and joy.

30

MY INNER CHILD
NEEDS OUT TO PLAY

Jesus called a little child to him and put the child among them.
Then he said, "I tell you the truth, unless you turn
from your sins and become like little children,
you will never get into the Kingdom of Heaven."

MATTHEW 18:2-3

When "Dad of Death" was being pummeled with decorative couch pillows by "Fearsome Faith" and "Pulverizing Paul" in Watkins Wrestling Mania, my wife would roll her eyes and refer to her *three* children. She probably had a point. Now that I'm a bit older—okay, a lot older—I can still act like a preschooler.

But I take comfort in the words of Jesus: "So anyone who becomes as humble as this little child is the greatest in the Kingdom of Heaven" (Matthew 18:4). Keeping our childlike spirit allows us to stay forever young! This is why:

Childlike adults are trusting. I love childlike trust in full force when grandchildren jump off the dresser, the edge of a pool, or the top of a wall, knowing that they are falling into the loving arms of a trusted Papaw.

King David wrote, "Cast your cares on the LORD and he will sustain you; he will never let the righteous be shaken" (Psalm 55:22, NIV). The Hebrew word *shalak*, translated with the word "cast" in that verse, literally means to throw, cast off, or toss out. Go ahead, jump off the dresser—metaphorically, of course—and throw the whole weight of your anxieties on God because he loves you unconditionally.

Do be aware of all the Social Security, home-repair, and IRS scams, but cultivating childlike trust in a God and people who love you will keep you young.

Childlike adults are innocent. Jesus told his listeners, "I tell you the truth, unless you turn from your sins and become like little children, you will never get into the Kingdom of Heaven" (Matthew 18:3). Sin ages us with its guilt, shame, and anxiety. Being able to live with clear consciences keeps us young.

Childlike adults are enthusiastic. There's a whole section on this, so moving right along . . .

Childlike adults are imaginative. Getting down on the floor with small children—even if you need help getting back up— is the best way to maintain your imagination. Everything is fresh and brand-new to a three-year-old, so soak in some of that perspective.

Childlike adults are creative. George Land's "Creativity Research Survey" conducted for NASA found that five-year-olds score 98 percent for creativity; ten-year-olds, 30 percent; fifteen-year-olds, 12 percent; and adults—wait for it—only 2 percent![48]

However, nothing brings out our inner child more than crayons, Play-Doh, and soap bubbles. And, of course, hanging around five-year-olds!

Childlike adults are curious. Again, there's a whole section on this important quality.

Childlikeness is essential for being a trusting, innocent, imaginative, creative, and curious child of God, although—disclaimer—there is a huge difference between childlike and childish. C. S. Lewis put it this way: "[God] wants a child's heart, but a grown-up's head."[49]

We live in an ironic society where even play is turned into work. But the highest existence is not work; the highest level of existence is play.
CONRAD HYERS

To Do
Select one of the childlike characteristics and look for ways to express it.

"He's been less gruff
since he's been on medication."

31

PRAISE THE LORD AND PASS THE PROZAC

The human spirit can endure a sick body,
but who can bear a crushed spirit?

PROVERBS 18:14

"Hi, I'm Jim. I have clinical depression." That probably comes as a shock to those who know me only as a humor writer and motivational speaker.

I've joked that my depression probably began at birth since my blood type is *B-negative*. I managed to plod through junior high—probably the source of all our deep-seated psychoses—high school, college, and several years as a youth pastor and then as a full-time speaker for children, youth, and adult conferences, camps, and churches, and finally, my dream job: working at a Christian publishing house.

I should have been happy. My wife, Lois, and I loved our jobs and had two wonderful kids in a Christian school, I was a published author and had earned national writing awards, and I was speaking all over the country. My tagline was actually "hope and humor"!

And yet it often took all my willpower to simply get out of bed. I got a lot of ministry done, but it felt like I was carrying a big, black boulder on my back that seemed to be getting heavier and heavier and heavier. I would drive past cemeteries and think, *Lucky stiffs*!

Unfortunately, I got absolutely no help from the church. I was told I should have more faith and quit my "stinkin' thinkin'." And to reinforce that I was spiritually defective, we sang, "I'm so happy and here's the reason why—Jesus took my burdens all away!" I wasn't . . . and he didn't!

It's biochemical

Fortunately, after I endured thirty years of suffering, a Christian doctor correctly diagnosed me and changed my life. He assured me that clinical depression was probably something I was born with. It was biochemical: a lack of serotonin and dopamine in my little brain. After trying three or four different anti-depressants, I finally found one with the best benefits and least side effects for me. Here's my encouragement for you:

You are not alone

First, if you're depressed, you're not a solo act. One in four people battle depression at some point. And you're in good company, joining Job, King David, the prophets Elijah and Jeremiah, as well as Martin Luther, C. S. Lewis, and Mother Teresa.

It may have *nothing* to do with you spiritually

Clinical depression is believed to be a chemical imbalance in the brain, not a spiritual dysfunction. It's a result of the Fall just as much as physical suffering and natural disasters. All the positive thoughts and prayers you can muster probably won't relieve it. So to those who tell me to just have more faith, I'd love to tell them, "And *you* need to have more faith for your diabetes, your blood pressure, and your ED!" Yeah . . . but I'm too nice to do that.

There is hope

With your doctor's help, you can find the right antidepressant for you.

However, a quick caveat: Meds are not a cure-all, but they do provide that extra mental strength to eat right, to exercise, and to think, as Paul writes, on those things that are true, honorable, right, pure, lovely, admirable, excellent, and praiseworthy (Philippians 4:8). *Depressing* is not on the list!

Also, there are licensed Christian therapists who can provide hope and help. I certainly needed counseling to shed years of guilt and shame heaped on me by previous churches.

In addition, you will find original articles and videos at www.jameswatkins.com/depression that I hope will be helpful. And if you ever need a sympathetic ear, email me at jim@jameswatkins.com. (No bots, no auto replies, no staff. Just me!)

So . . . Hi, I'm Jim. I have clinical depression. And I have hope and joy in Jesus Christ!

> *Maybe you have to know the darkness*
> *before you can appreciate the light.*
> MADELEINE L'ENGLE

To Do

If you feel depressed for no apparent reason for two weeks or more, see your primary care physician.

PART IX

OPTIMISM

Made a willful, deliberate decision to turn negative thinking about aging into positive thoughts based on God's love and promise for his "good, pleasing and perfect will."

Do not be afraid or discouraged.
For the LORD your God is with you wherever you go.

JOSHUA 1:9

32

ON JUPITER, I'M JUST FIVE YEARS OLD

For everything there is a season,
a time for every activity under heaven.

ECCLESIASTES 3:1

Because it takes Jupiter 4,333 Earth days to orbit the sun,[50] I would be just five years old on the gaseous planet. However, because the gravitational pull is more than two and a half times stronger on Jupiter,[51] I'd also weigh over four hundred pounds. And a four-hundred-pound five-year-old waiting nearly twelve Earth years for Christmas would not be a good thing. Oh, and there's no oxygen, so it's really not a viable plan for turning back the clock.

While I can't do anything about the act of aging, I can do something about acting *aged*! Rather than thinking of myself as sixty-nine years old, I prefer to think of myself as a twenty-nine-year-old with forty years' experience.

So please repeat after me the ninth characteristic of Agers Anonymous on optimism: "Made a willful, deliberate decision to turn negative thinking about aging into positive thoughts based on God's love and promise for his 'good, pleasing and perfect will.'"

First, as Albert Einstein claimed . . .

Our time on Earth is relative. The Bible says, "You must not forget this one thing, dear friends: A day is like a thousand years to the Lord, and a thousand years is like a day" (2 Peter 3:8).

Based on God's perspective, either my great-grandparents have not been born yet or I'm over twenty-five million years old! (I sometimes feel old, but never *that* old.)

Our time on Earth is unpredictable. Christ teaches an important parable about a rich man who builds larger barns to hold his plentiful harvest, then sits back and says to himself: "'My friend, you have enough stored away for years to come. Now take it easy! Eat, drink, and be merry!' But God said to him, 'You fool! You will die this very night. Then who will get everything you worked for?'" (Luke 12:19-20).

And from Psalm 89:47: "Remember how short my life is."

Our time on Earth is perfectly planned by God. No matter how long or short your life is, God has a plan—and you're not leaving until it is accomplished. Remember, if you're not dead, you're not done.

For we are God's masterpiece. He has created us
anew in Christ Jesus, so we can do the good things
he planned for us long ago.

EPHESIANS 2:10

My future is in your hands.

PSALM 31:15

We can make our plans, but the LORD determines
our steps.

PROVERBS 16:9

Followers of Christ should be the most optimistic people
on planet Earth. God has a "good, pleasing and perfect" plan
for our brief time here (Romans 12:2, NIV).

*My physical body may be less efficient and less beautiful
in old age. But God has given me a vast compensation:
my mind is richer, my experience is wealthier,
my soul is broader, and my wisdom is at a peak.*

ROBERT MULLER

To Do

Relax. You're not going anywhere
unless God says so.

"Who?"

33

YOU'RE NO LONGER A SPRING CHICKEN, BUT YOU *ARE* A WISE OLD OWL

*Wisdom belongs to the aged,
and understanding to the old.*

JOB 12:12

My granddaughters love to play get-to-know-you games, such as "Would You Rather?" Some of the questions in that game are thought-provoking: "Would you rather be loved or be feared?" And some, not so much: "Would you rather have a constantly dripping nose or never-ending diarrhea?"

When they were four and six years old, another game gave the three of us an assignment: "Describe each person with one word." The oldest thought her younger sister was "silly." I preferred "creative." Little sister thought big sister was "bossy." I described her as "thoughtful." (She asks the best questions!)

I was holding my breath for their descriptions of me. True to form, my youngest thought I was "goofy." However, my thoughtful granddaughter surprised me with "intelligent." I was shocked!

"Really?"

"Yeah. You always have good answers to my questions, Papaw."

I pray that is always the case. I've noticed my relationship with my kids and my grandkiddos changed as they matured. From goofy "playmate" to "intelligent" friend. I love it when my adult children call me for advice.

Yep, I'm no longer a spring chicken, but I'm becoming a wise old owl. The anonymous author of Psalm 71 writes:

Now that I am old and gray,
do not abandon me, O God.
Let me proclaim your power to this new generation,
your mighty miracles to all who come after me.

PSALM 71:18

When my children were teenagers, I wrote three books based on twenty-five hundred junior high and senior high students' questions about sex, death, and the supernatural. It's been encouraging to see my adult children now use those books to answer their children's questions. In fact, ten of my twenty-plus books were penned for young people as my own children grew up.

You may not be writing books, but Bible truths are being taught through your life and settling in the hearts and minds of your children and grandchildren. It's something God urges us to do:

> Commit yourselves wholeheartedly to these words of mine. Tie them to your hands and wear them on your forehead as reminders. Teach them to your children. Talk about them when you are at home and when you are on the road, when you are going to bed and when you are getting up. Write them on the doorposts of your house and on your gates, so that as long as the sky remains above the earth, you and your children may flourish.

DEUTERONOMY 11:18-21

> *Knowledge comes from learning.*
> *Wisdom comes from living.*
> ANTHONY DOUGLAS WILLIAMS

To Do

Write out your favorite memories— along with lessons learned— for your children and grandchildren.

"Our marriage is one
good news/bad news joke."

34

THAT'S GOOD— THAT'S BAD

*We know that in all things God works for the good
of those who love him, who have been called according
to his purpose . . . to be conformed to the image of his Son.*

ROMANS 8:28-29, NIV

God is the originator of the old "good news/bad news" joke, and Romans 8:28-29 is the punch line.

While giving birth to Faith, our first child, Lois vomited during delivery and inhaled her stomach contents. The previous three patients with aspiration pneumonia at the hospital had died, so Lois was rushed to ICU, unable to see her brand-new daughter. For five long days, we waited to see if Lois would live. It was certainly a bad situation.

The church-provided health insurance paid a pittance for childbirth. It did, however, supply full major medical coverage. The birth of our daughter, which would have cost us thousands of dollars, was now paid in full because Lois was in ICU. That's good!

Throughout our lives, we have seen hundreds of examples in our lives and others when weeping turned to laughter.

156 || IF YOU'RE NOT DEAD, YOU'RE NOT DONE

But to be honest, I'm not always laughing. In fact, I seem to go through a three-D process. A few years ago, Lois and I had a financial setback, which immediately sent me into full-blown crisis mode triggering the first D:

Doubt

I wish there was a more flattering word for it, but for about a week, I *doubted* that God had a plan and that he was working for our good to provide for us. I felt it was up to *me* to keep my family from living in a cardboard box! I frantically brainstormed ways to cut expenses and generate more income: sell my books on the street corner, pawn my guitars, and give up dark chocolate.

Decide

During week two, I finally got a grip. (The thought of giving up dark chocolate brought me to my senses.)

God had been there during more than forty years of faith ministry and had always provided unexpected income, whether from jobs and projects that appeared from seemingly nowhere to surprising inheritances from family and friends. I willfully and deliberately decided to trust that God would do the same this time as well. White-knuckle trust is better than yellow-bellied doubt, right?

Delight

However, King David described a higher level of faith than simply trust: "Trust in the LORD and do good. Then you will live safely in the land and prosper. Take *delight* in the LORD, and he will give you your heart's desires" (Psalm 37:3-4, my emphasis).

Week three brought joyful anticipation. I had made a list of all the surprising ways God had pulled a rabbit out of the hat in the past when everything looked black and empty. I actually broke into my happy dance. I couldn't wait to see what miracle—not magic trick—God was going to perform in turning good out of bad. And of course, as you've already discovered, he did!

> *When God closes a door . . . he just knocks out the whole*
> *side of a house and opens up an amazing view.*
> FAITH A. WATKINS, MY DAUGHTER

To Do

Make a list of all the ways God has worked good out of bad in your life.

"Remember, Mr. Murphey,
there's always a purpose in pain.
In your case, to pay off my lake house."

35

PAIN IS GOD'S MEGAPHONE

He comforts us in all our troubles so that we can comfort others.
When they are troubled, we will be able to
give them the same comfort God has given us.

2 CORINTHIANS 1:4

Remember my mentioning the excruciating pain of a kidney stone? My kidney would have failed within a few days if God hadn't put half of my pain and pleasure receptors in my plumbing. Normally, it takes arterial bleeding or a compound fracture to send me to the doctor, but within half an hour, I was out of our warm bed, into the cold November night, dashing through the snow, and peeing into a paper cup at the ER.

And since I was tethered to an IV pole, I had a lot of time to think and journal about pain.

Pain produces perspective. Although I had a deadline for my weekly newspaper column the next day and was finishing up a book, those things were suddenly at the bottom of my to-do list.

The experience provided a whole new way of looking at life. Very little fazes me now, since I can say, "Sure beats a kidney stone!"

Pain produces perseverance. The New Testament recounts that the apostle Paul was given the power to heal the sick and raise the dead. Pretty impressive pain relief! But somehow, God chose not to heal Paul's own "thorn in the flesh." Now if I were Paul, I'd be pretty discouraged. Instead, he wrote:

> Since we have been made right in God's sight by faith, we have peace with God because of what Jesus Christ our Lord has done for us. Because of our faith, Christ has brought us into this place of undeserved privilege where we now stand, and we confidently and joyfully look forward to sharing God's glory.
>
> We can rejoice, too, when we run into problems and trials, for we know that they help us develop endurance. And endurance develops strength of character, and character strengthens our confident hope of salvation.
>
> ROMANS 5:1-4

The most positive, loving people I know have histories of great emotional or physical pain and yet they have persevered. As Kelly Clarkson sang, "What doesn't kill you makes you stronger." But first, it's going to hurt like bloody murder!

Pain produces purpose. I can hear you thinking, *Okay, Mister Smarty-Pants Author, what is God's role in pain? Does he cause our pain? Or does he allow tragedies? Or is he simply vacationing in Cancún and hasn't checked his voice mail recently?*

I can say with the utmost confidence—and I have a degree in theology and an ordination certificate—I don't have a clue! I really don't. I do know, however, that whether God causes, allows, or simply takes a hands-off approach to pain, he does somehow personally, lovingly, miraculously redeem it for our good.

God has used physical pain to move me past annoyance with old people's complaints ("Come on, Gramps, stop obsessing about your colon!") to a real empathy for anyone in pain. Yep, God even works together stubborn kidney stones for good!

> *Pain insists upon being attended to. God whispers to us in our pleasures, speaks in our conscience, but shouts in our pain. It is his megaphone to rouse a deaf world.*
>
> C. S. LEWIS

To Do

Reflect on what lessons you have learned and how you've become a better person through pain.

"Not again!"

36
ALL'S NOT LOST WITH ALZHEIMER'S

I am certain that God, who began the good work within you,
will continue his work until it is finally finished
on the day when Christ Jesus returns.

PHILIPPIANS 1:6

A dreadful poem, attributed to the Alzheimer's Association, is being spread across social networks in which the author laments, "The best of me is gone." Wrong! Wrong! Wrong! This couldn't be farther from the truth!

Your best is in your children and grandchildren.

If you are experiencing early-onset Alzheimer's, here's the good news. The best of you lives on in your children and grandchildren. They carry your DNA and, in many ways, your personality.

A lifetime of your influence, encouragement, and life lessons as well as the values and beliefs you modeled will live on in your family well beyond your years. The best of you is not gone!

Your best is in your friends, coworkers, students, customers . . .

Unless since birth, you've lived alone on a deserted island, the best of you lives on in those for whom you have offered help, taught a skill or life lesson, or provided a valuable service. Your advice, admonitions, teaching, and mentoring will continue throughout their lives and the lives they influence. The best of you is not gone!

Your best is in the lives your faith has touched

For followers of Jesus suffering from Alzheimer's, a lifetime of modeling your faith before family and friends has impacted the very Kingdom of God. If you have served as a Sunday school teacher, preacher, missionary, or faithful layperson, your best lives on in the eternally changed lives of those you served. The best of you is not gone!

Your best is in you right now!

If you are further down the path of Alzheimer's, you may not know today's date, recognize old friends, or even remember your spouse. He or she is simply a nice person who comes to see you each day. That nice person may be reading this devotional to you right now.

But even as your mind leaves this earth well before your body, it stands as a monument for what you stood for. It's a reminder of the love and influence you poured out on your family and friends. Think of yourself as a living photograph—it may be silent—and yet it speaks love, faith, and courage. Your good work is not finished! And the best of you is not gone!

The best is yet to be

"On the day when Christ Jesus returns" you will be perfectly restored in mind and body. Jesus himself will greet you with the words "Well done, good and faithful servant." So even as you are dying to this world, eternal life awaits you. And in heaven, the dying memories of this world will be resurrected as you reunite with family and friends who have gone before you. The best of you is just beginning as you make the transition from earthly memories to eternal reality!

The things we do are like monuments that
people build to honor heroes after they've died. . . .
Only instead of being made out of stone,
they're made out of the memories people have of you.

R. J. PALACIO

To Do

Remember this: Your fading memories will be fully restored when Christ returns.

PART X

SIGNIFICANCE

Having experienced a spiritual
awakening and been energized
with God's power, we tried to
live out these characteristics
each day of our lives.

Some parts of the body that seem weakest and least
important are actually the most necessary. And the parts
we regard as less honorable are those we clothe with the
greatest care. So we carefully protect those parts that
should not be seen, while the more honorable parts do
not require this special care. So God has put the body
together such that extra honor and care are given
to those parts that have less dignity.

1 CORINTHIANS 12:22-24

GRANDMA MOSES

37

NO EXPIRATION DATE

Moses was eighty years old, and Aaron was eighty-three
when they made their demands to Pharaoh.

EXODUS 7:7

You may be retired and collecting Social Security, but that doesn't mean that your years of significant and productive work are finished.

Harland Sanders was old enough to draw Medicare benefits when he cooked up KFC. Noah Webster compiled his *American Dictionary of the English Language* at age seventy.[52]

Roget created the thesaurus at the ancient, antiquated, full, hoary, mature, ripe, and timeworn old age of seventy-three.[53] Anna Mary Robertson Moses, aka Grandma Moses, started painting at age seventy-six because arthritis had crippled her hands so that she no longer could embroider.[54] John Glenn, the first American to orbit the earth, returned to space at seventy-seven for experiments on the effects of space on aging.[55]

Evangelist Billy Graham preached his last crusade, before 242,000 people over three days, in New York City[56] at eighty-six. He continued writing until his death at just short of one hundred.

And keep in mind, as mentioned earlier, "Moses was 120 years old when he died, yet his eyesight was clear, and he was as strong as ever" (Deuteronomy 34:7).

So, what's on your to-do list for today? It may not be starting a billion-dollar business, or speaking to thousands of people, or going into space, but you can change your world today!

You can encourage staff and servers at your assisted living home.

You can send an email, enter a post on Facebook, or use an old-school card, envelope, and stamp to provide hope to a friend or family member.

You can start an email newsletter for family and friends sharing family news and encouragement. My sister-in-love, who is thirteen years my elder, faithfully sends out daily emails with Scripture and inspiring quotations.

You can be paralyzed and on a ventilator but still pray for your family, your medical staff, your fellow patients, your pastor and church, your city, state, country, and world. Most important, you can praise God. (In Revelation 19:4, four "creatures" and twenty-four elders apparently do nothing except surround God's throne and praise him.)

Remember, if you woke up this morning, God has something eternally meaningful, purposeful, and significant for you to do. Howard and William Hendricks write in their book, *As Iron Sharpens Iron*: "Paul likened the Christian life to a race. . . . Unfortunately for many of us, the longer we run, the less energy we have to finish well. Some of us are fading in the stretch. . . . As a result, many . . . over fifty-five are . . . sliding for home."[57]

I never want to be "sliding for home." Whether I am running full out—or limping and staggering—into the arms of Jesus, I want to finish the race! I pray you want that too. Because if you're not dead, you're not done!

> *I suppose real old age begins when one looks*
> *backward rather than forward.*
>
> MAY SARTON

To Do

Change your corner of the world—today!

"Isn't that idle worship?"

38
NO LOITERING!

To me, living means living for Christ, and dying is even better.
But if I live, I can do more fruitful work for Christ.
So I really don't know which is better. I'm torn between two desires:
I long to go and be with Christ, which would be far better for me.

PHILIPPIANS 1:21-23

David Brainerd, the famous missionary to Native Americans, struggled like Paul, being "torn between two desires." Both men longed to serve here on earth, but they also believed dying and going to the One they served "would be far better."

All during his time of ministry, Brainerd was suffering both physically and psychologically. He struggled with tuberculosis as well as being tormented with what would be diagnosed today as clinical depression. His journal is filled with his desire to serve God, but he often believed he was only serving time.

> [I] was scarce ever more confounded with a sense
> of my own unfruitfulness and unfitness of my
> work, than now. Oh, what a dead, heartless, barren,

unprofitable wretch did I now see myself to be!
My spirits were so low, and my bodily strength
so wasted, that I could do nothing at all.[58]

Over twenty times in his journal he cries out for death to take him. "I longed for death exceedingly."[59] Yet, in spite of his physical and mental torment, Brainerd had an effective ministry with indigenous people. He also heavily influenced famous preacher Jonathan Edwards as he spent his dying days in Edwards's home, and he is credited for inspiring the founding of Yale and Dartmouth Universities. His raw and vulnerable journal, *The Life of David Brainerd*, has encouraged generations of missionaries to soldier on, in spite of their own challenges. (The book, compiled by Edwards after Brainerd's death, is still in print and continues to minister to current generations of missionaries.)

John Piper writes, "Brainerd's life is a vivid, powerful testimony to the truth that God can and does use weak, sick, discouraged, beat-down, lonely, struggling saints, who cry to him day and night, to accomplish amazing things for his glory."[60]

Through his struggles, Brainerd kept striving to serve the God he had come to know and love just eight years earlier. "O I longed to fill the remaining moments all for God! Though my body was so feeble, and wearied with preaching and much private conversation, yet I wanted to sit up all night to do something for God. To God the giver of these refreshments, be glory forever and ever; Amen."[61]

His four years as a missionary ended in 1747 when he died of tuberculosis at just twenty-nine years old. But David Brainerd's prayers were answered: "Oh, that I might not loiter on my heavenly journey!"[62]

He embodied Paul's words: "Make the most of every opportunity" (Ephesians 5:16) and "Let's not get tired of doing what is good. At just the right time we will reap a harvest of blessing if we don't give up" (Galatians 6:9).

> *I do not want my life to be extended if it would mean*
> *that I should cease to live right and fail in my mission*
> *to glorify You all of my days! I would rather go home*
> *right now than to live on—if living on was*
> *to be a waste of God's time and my own.*
>
> A. W. TOZER

To Do

"Make the most of every opportunity."

"Don't worry, Mr. Thorson.
Soon you'll be transformed
into a butterfly."

39

WHEN YOU CAN'T DO
A BLESSED THING

We were crushed and overwhelmed beyond our ability to endure,
and we thought we would never live through it.
In fact, we expected to die. But as a result,
we stopped relying on ourselves and learned to rely only on God.

2 CORINTHIANS 1:8-9

In *To Kill a Mockingbird*, Jem tells his younger sister, Scout, that their father "is real old, but I wouldn't care if he couldn't do anything—I wouldn't care if he couldn't do a blessed thing."[63]

I'm sure that's the sentiment our Father feels toward his children: "I don't care if they can't do a blessed thing." God's love for us is not based on what we can or cannot do, but on his unbelievable, unconditional, unfathomable love toward us. And so, this chapter is written for those who feel they can't do a blessed thing.

Perhaps you have congestive heart failure and are tethered to an oxygen tank and have the strength only to be assisted to and from the bathroom. Maybe you're flat on your back with failing vision and a loved one or staff member is reading this chapter to you. Or you may be like my friend Bill Sweeney, who writes an inspiring blog offering *Unshakable Hope*.

> At the age of thirty-five, I was diagnosed with Amyotrophic Lateral Sclerosis (ALS or "Lou Gehrig's Disease"). I'm now completely paralyzed and unable to speak. I'm writing this using a special computer that allows me to type using eye movements like Stephen Hawking.
>
> The only thing I'm physically able to do is type, and I want to encourage believers that God really can bring them through any trial; I know what it's like to get a terminal diagnosis, to lose a good job, to be drowning in debt, and to battle depression, etc.
>
> I don't believe God causes trials, but he clearly does allow them for reasons I don't believe we will ever fully understand—at least not in this life. . . .
>
> This trial has taught us that the only way to experience genuine and consistent hope, peace and joy in the midst of a trial is to view our life and situation through God's eyes. For me, learning this was a long and difficult, but rewarding process; an ongoing process that will continue to the day I go to be with God. I simply want to encourage people.
>
> I've become convinced that for a Christian to retain *hope* in the midst of a difficult trial, he or she

must believe that God *allowed* the trial for a purpose; a purpose greater than what God would have been able to accomplish in and through that person apart from the trial . . . (Romans 8:28). . . .

A difficult trial (usually) causes the Christian to focus more on the spiritual and the eternal things because, by comparison, the temporal and the material things begin to look more and more insignificant.[64]

Bill has learned that even when you can't do a blessed thing, you can still bless God and be a blessing to others. You can praise God. You can pray. And even if you can only communicate with your eyes like Bill, you can still share your faith with the world.

> *Helplessness is your best prayer.*
> *It calls from your heart to the heart of God*
> *with greater effect than all your uttered pleas.*
> OLE HALLESBY

To Do

Love God. That's all he asks of you!

"She can't come to the phone
right now. She's busy leaving
her mark on the world."

40

YOU WILL LEAVE A HOLE—AND NOT JUST IN THE GROUND

You have become an example to all the believers.

1 THESSALONIANS 1:7

My very favorite movie of all time is the 1946 Christmas classic *It's a Wonderful Life*. The film stars Jimmy Stewart as George Bailey, an aspiring world-traveling adventurer. Unfortunately, his dreams are shattered as he is forced to take over his late father's savings and loan in the "crummy little town" of Bedford Falls.

On Christmas Eve, with the loan company facing ruin and scandal, George decides to end his life by jumping into the freezing river. But before he can commit suicide, Clarence Oddbody: Angel Second Class, dives in the river, causing George to save the angel's life—and his own.

And—spoiler alert, if you're the only person in the Milky Way galaxy who has not seen the movie—Clarence shows George what life would be for his wife, his family, the savings and loan, Bedford Falls, and the entire WWII effort without George in it.

As George watches in horror, Clarence delivers the key line of the film: "Strange, isn't it? Each man's life touches so many other lives and when he isn't around he leaves an awful hole, doesn't he?"

We have all had our George Bailey moment when we wondered if we've made any difference in our world. And as we live out our Act III, it's easy to become discouraged.

Let's go back to our very first portion of Scripture.

Therefore we do not lose heart. Though outwardly we are wasting away, yet inwardly we are being renewed day by day. For our light and momentary troubles are achieving for us an eternal glory that far outweighs them all. So we fix our eyes not on what is seen, but on what is unseen, since what is seen is temporary, but what is unseen is eternal.

2 CORINTHIANS 4:16-18, NIV

George Bailey was seeing only temporal things: "I want to do something big and something important. . . . I'm gonna build things. I'm gonna build airfields, I'm gonna build sky-scrapers a hundred stories high, I'm gonna build bridges a mile long."

But nothing—zip, zero, zilch—on this earth will last for

eternity, except for eternal souls and the influence we have had on them.

You may not have a lot of earthly treasures in your down-sized retirement house or single room at the assisted living center, but there is a world of invaluable goods that will live on in the lives you have influenced as you pass through this life. So "set your sights on the realities of heaven. . . . Think about the things of heaven, not the things of earth" (Colossians 3:1-2).

And then you'll be able to say, as Clarence did, "You really had a wonderful life."

If you want to be of use to God, maintain the proper relationship with Jesus Christ by staying focused on Him, and He will make use of you every minute you live—yet you will be unaware, on the conscious level of your life, that you are being used of Him.

OSWALD CHAMBERS

To Do

Make a list of everyone you have had an eternal influence upon. Then thank God for your wonderful life.

ACKNOWLEDGMENTS

No one writes a book on their own. It's always a collaboration of family, friends, and influencers who have contributed to the pages of our lives. Thank you to the "authors" who have enriched my story with their love, example, and wisdom. In alphabetical order, they are Elsie Drummonds; Jimmy Johnson; my parents, Donald and Barbara Watkins; my wife, Lois; Dick Wynn; and Bob Zuhl. You helped write each word of this book.

And to my friends and fellow authors who offered comments and constructive criticism for this specific book: Wenda Clements, Paula Geister, Beth Jacobs, Jerry B. Jenkins, Lissa Halls Johnson, John Latta, Marie Latta, Janice Miller, Cec Murphey, Cheryl Walker, David Winters, and Marcia Woodard.

And of course, the wonderful people at Tyndale House whose editorial skills made my writing so much better than what I originally turned in: Becky Brandvik, Bonne Steffen, and Annette Hayward. Thanks also to Jonny Hawkins for his witty and wacky cartoons, and to Libby Dykstra for her delightful design of the cover and interior pages.

I am eternally grateful to each of you.

NOTES

1. Emily Hourican, "She Wasn't an Enigma, She Was a Drunk," Independ.ie, March 6, 2017, https://www.independent.ie/entertainment/she-wasnt-an -enigma-she-was-a-drunk-35499968.html.
2. Romans 12:2, NIV.
3. Ullah Asmat, Khan Abad, and Khan Ismail, "Diabetes Mellitus and Oxidative Stress—A Concise Review," *Saudi Pharmaceutical Journal* 24, no. 5 (September 2016), 547–53, https://doi.org/10.1016/j.jsps.2015.03.013.
4. Elizabeth Arias and Jiaquan Xu, "United States Life Tables, 2017," National Vital Statistics Reports vol. 68, no. 7 (June 24, 2019), 3.
5. Quoted in Jennifer Soong, "The Secret (and Surprising) Power of Naps," WebMD Magazine, 2010, https://www.webmd.com/balance/features /the-secret-and-surprising-power-of-naps#1.
6. Lisa Stein, "Napping May Be Good for Your Heart," *Scientific American*, February 12, 2007, https://www.scientificamerican.com/article/napping -good-for-heart/.
7. Sara Mednick, *Take a Nap! Change Your Life* (New York: Workman Publishing, 2006).
8. Quoted in John Leland, "Reading, Walking and More Reading for Writer," *New York Times*, November 15, 2013, https://www.nytimes.com/2013 /11/17/nyregion/reading-walking-and-more-reading-for-writer.html.
9. "Why You Need a Nana Nap," *Sydney Morning Herald*, July 8, 2013, https:// www.smh.com.au/lifestyle/why-you-need-a-nana-nap-20130704-2pf4n.html.
10. Mednick, *Take a Nap!*
11. "Sometimes You Just Need a Nap and a Snack," *Real Life LA*, a blog of Real Life Church, http://www.reallife.la/blog/2017/1/27/sometimes-you -just-need-a-nap-and-a-snack.

12. Dorothy West, *The Wedding* (New York: Anchor Books, 1996), 171.

13. Crombie Jardine, *The Best Dorothy Parker Quotes* (n.p.: Crombie Jardine Publishing, 2016).

14. Margery Williams, *The Velveteen Rabbit, or How Toys Become Real* (New York: Derrydale Books, 1986), 14–15.

15. Jay Warner, *American Singing Groups: A History from 1940 to Today* (Milwaukee: Hal Leonard, 2006), 514.

16. Quoted in Kathy Parker, "Grief Is Just Love with No Place to Go," *This Girl Unravelled* (blog), accessed March 8, 2021, https://kathyparker.com .au/2017/01/02/grief-is-just-love-with-no-place-to-go/.

17. Paul Pearsall, *Super Marital Sex: Loving for Life* (New York: Doubleday, 1987), 98.

18. "Guide to Sex after 60," WebMD, accessed September 4, 2020, https:// www.webmd.com/healthy-aging/ss/slideshow-guide-to-sex-after-60.

19. Samuel Ullman, "Youth," Samuel Ullman Museum website, https://www .uab.edu/ullmanmuseum/.

20. From an essay by Bessie Anderson Stanley of Lincoln, Kansas. An article about her essay appeared in the *Emporia Gazette* (Emporia, Kansas) on December 11, 1905, https://quoteinvestigator.com/2012/06/26/define -success/#:~:text=%E2%80%9CTo%20laugh%20often%20and%20 much,a%20garden%20patch%2C%20or%20a.

21. Harold Kushner, *When All You've Ever Wanted Isn't Enough* (New York: Simon and Schuster, 2002), 20.

22. Louise L. Looney and James N. Watkins, *Over the Hill . . . Onto the Mountaintop* (Nashville, TN: ACW Press, 2014).

23. "Longevity in the Ancient World," Early Church History website, accessed December 29, 2020, https://earlychurchhistory.org/daily-life/longevity-in -the-ancient-world/.

24. Quoted in Donald Vickery, Larry Matson, and Carol Vickery, *Live Young, Think Young, Be Young, . . . at Any Age* (Boulder, CO: Bull Publishing, 2012), 285.

25. Nicholas Murray, *Aldous Huxley: A Biography* (New York: St. Martin's Press, 2003), 414.

26. Christopher Bergland, "Curiosity and Conscientiousness More Important than Intelligence," *Psychology Today*, December 7, 2011, https://www .psychologytoday.com/us/blog/the-athletes-way/201112/curiosity-and -conscientiousness-more-important-intelligence, emphasis in the original.

27. Quoted in Bette R. Bonder and Vanina Dal Bello-Haas, *Functional Performance in Older Adults* (Philadelphia: E. A. Davis Company, 2009), iv.

28. "Learning Helps Keep Brain Healthy," UCI News, March 2, 2010, https://news.uci.edu/2010/03/02/uc-irvine-news-release-learning-helps-keep-brain-healthy/.

29. "Learning Helps Keep Brain Healthy."

30. Romeo Vitelli, "Can Lifelong Learning Help as We Age?," *Psychology Today*, October 14, 2012, https://www.psychologytoday.com/us/blog/media-spotlight/201210/can-lifelong-learning-help-we-age#:~:text=Gerontological%20research%20has%20shown%20that,of%20U3A%20students%20remain%20scarce.

31. Penny Dacks, "Cognitive Enrichment: Lifelong Learning May Help Prevent Dementia," Cognitive Vitality, June 30, 2014, https://www.alzdiscovery.org/cognitive-vitality/blog/cognitive-enrichment.

32. "Lifelong Learning," Valamis website, accessed September 4, 2020, https://www.valamis.com/hub/lifelong-learning.

33. "How Life-Long Learning Will Benefit You," *Psychologies*, May 2, 2014, https://www.psychologies.co.uk/how-life-long-learning-will-benefit-you.

34. "New Plastic Surgery Statistics Reveal Trends toward Body Enhancement," American Society of Plastic Surgeons, *Cision*, March 11, 2019, https://www.prnewswire.com/news-releases/new-plastic-surgery-statistics-reveal-trends-toward-body-enhancement-300809272.html.

35. "Facelift Guide," American Board of Cosmetic Surgery, accessed September 4, 2020, https://www.americanboardcosmeticsurgery.org/procedure-learning-center/face/facelift-guide/.

36. Yvette Brazier, "Facelift: What You Need to Know," Medical News Today (newsletter), March 31, 2017, https://www.medicalnewstoday.com/articles/244066.

37. Brazier, "Facelift."

38. Timothy McGee, "How Long Does a Facelift Last?," Westlake Dermatology website, April 3, 2018, https://www.westlakedermatology.com/blog/how-long-does-a-facelift-last/.

39. "How Much Does a Facelift Cost?" Dermatology & Plastic Surgery of Arizona, February 6, 2020, https://www.dermplasticsaz.com/blog/how-much-does-facelift-cost/.

40. "Facelift Surgery—Costs, Risks & Recovery," Consumer Guide to Plastic Surgery, accessed September 4, 2020, https://www.yourplasticsurgeryguide.com/face-lift/cost/.

41. Edzard Ernst, "Alternative Practitioners Amuse the Patient, While Medics Cure the Disease," *Journal of Clinical Medicine* 7, no. 6 (June 2018), 137, https://doi.org/10.3390/jcm7060137.

42. Dark chocolate has been shown in major studies to improve the function of blood vessels (European Society of Cardiology), increase blood flow to the brain and improve scores on memory and thinking skill tests (*Neurology*), increase mental skills (Syracuse University), and decrease heart disease, cancer, and other health conditions (*The Lancet*). Sorry, milk and white chocolate show no healthy benefits.

43. Don Colburn, "Norman Cousins, Still Laughing," *Washington Post*, October 21, 1986, https://www.washingtonpost.com/archive/lifestyle /wellness/1986/10/21/norman-cousins-still-laughing/e17f23cb-3e8c -4f58-b907-2dcd00326e22/.

44. Quoted in Karen Siugzda, "Benefits of Laughing Even When You Don't Feel Like It," Laughter Wellness with Karen, October 16, 2015, http:// www.laughterwellnesswithkaren.com/blog/2015/10/16/benefits-of -laughing-even-when-you-dont-feel-like-it/.

45. Association for Applied and Therapeutic Humor, https://www.aath.org /about-aath.

46. Anne Lamott, *Small Victories: Spotting Improbable Moments of Grace* (New York: Riverhead Books, 2014), 51.

47. Ashley Abramson, "Holding a Grudge Can Make You Sick," Elemental, November 20, 2019, https://elemental.medium.com/holding-a-grudge -can-make-you-sick-5179ed066e11.

48. George Land, "The Failure of Success," filmed December 2010 in Tucson, AZ, and posted February 16, 2011, TEDx video, 6:45–8:16, https://www .youtube.com/watch?v=ZfKMq-rYtnc&feature=emb_title.

49. C. S. Lewis, *Mere Christianity* (New York: Macmillan, 1952), 75.

50. "How Long Is a Year on Other Planets?" Space Place, NASA Science, last updated July 13, 2020, https://spaceplace.nasa.gov/years-on-other-planets /en/.

51. "Gravity on Earth, Jupiter and Pluto," Bitesize, BBC, accessed September 8, 2020, https://www.bbc.co.uk/bitesize/clips/zcbmyrd.

52. "The History of Webster's Dictionary," American Dictionary of the English Language website, http://webstersdictionary1828.com/NoahWebster.

53. *Encyclopaedia Britannica Online*, s.v. "Peter Mark Roget," accessed September 9, 2010, https://www.britannica.com/biography/Peter-Mark -Roget.

54. Olivia B. Waxman, "Grandma Moses Didn't Start Painting until Her 70s. Here's Why," *Time*, September 7, 2016, https://time.com/4482257/grandma-moses-history/.

55. Valerie Neal, "John Glenn's Return to Space on *Discovery*," Smithsonian National Air and Space Museum website, October 29, 2018, https://airandspace.si.edu/stories/editorial/john-glenns-return-space-discovery.

56. "Crusade City Spotlight: Greater New York City, June 24, 2015," Billy Graham Library blog, www.billygrahamlibrary.org/crusade-city-spotlight-greater-new-york-city/.

57. Howard and William Hendricks, *As Iron Sharpens Iron* (Chicago: Moody Publishers, 1995), 149.

58. John Piper, *David Brainerd: May I Never Loiter on My Heavenly Journey!* (Minneapolis: Desiring God Foundation, 2012), 13.

59. Piper, 13.

60. Piper, 9.

61. Piper, 21.

62. Piper, 21.

63. Harper Lee, *To Kill a Mockingbird* (New York: Harper Perennial, 2002), chapter 10.

64. Bill Sweeney, "Why Me?" *Unshakable Hope*, June 14, 2013, https://unshakablehope.com/2013/06/14/why-me/.

TWO WHO AREN'T
DONE YET

James Watkins is an award-winning author of more than twenty books and thousands of articles, as well as a popular speaker at churches, colleges, and conferences. He taught writing at Taylor University for fifteen years and was a guest lecturer at Liberty, Regent, and other universities. His goal is to continue doing what he loves to do until at least his hundredth birthday.

Jonny Hawkins is a full-time cartoonist whose work has appeared in more than 900 publications, including *Reader's Digest*, *Parade*, and *Guideposts*. He has drawn more than 50,000 cartoons, published 20 books, and created 76 page-a-day calendars.

OTHER BOOKS BY JAMES N. WATKINS

Overcoming Fear and Worry

God, I Don't Understand: Unanswered Prayer,
Unfulfilled Promises, and Unpunished Evil

The Imitation of Christ: Classic Devotions in Today's Language

Squeezing Good Out of Bad

Follow Jim at jameswatkins.com